Grammar for College Writing

For Jenny, a model for all that is good to imitate.
With love, Don

For Don, whose kindness, generosity, and perpetual growth are inspirational.
With love, Jenny

"I wanted to write, and I did not even know the English language. I bought English grammars and found them dull. I felt that I was getting a better sense of the language from novels than grammars."
—Richard Wright, *Black Boy*

****

"Perhaps it is time to return to grammar [through novels and other literature]."
—C. S. Lewis, *The Chronicles of Narnia*

Grammar for College Writing

A Sentence-Composing Approach— A Student Worktext

DON and JENNY KILLGALLON

Boynton/Cook Publishers
HEINEMANN
Portsmouth, NH

Heinemann

361 Hanover Street

Portsmouth, NH 03801–3912

www.boyntoncook.com

Offices and agents throughout the world

Library of Congress Cataloging-in-Publication Data

Killgallon, Don.

  Grammar for college writing : a sentence-composing approach : a student worktext / Don and Jenny Killgallon.

      p. cm.

   ISBN-13: 978-0-86709-602-6

   ISBN-10: 0-86709-602-0

  1. English language—Grammar—Problems, exercises, etc. 2. English language—Sentences—Problems, exercises, etc. 3. English language—Rhetoric—Problems, exercises, etc. 4. Report writing—Problems, exercises, etc.

I. Killgallon, Jenny. II. Title.

   PE1413.K456   2010

   428.2076—dc22   2009038590

Editor: Lisa Luedeke
Production: Elizabeth Valway
Cover design: Shawn Girsberger
Composition: House of Equations, Inc.
Manufacturing: Steve Bernier

Printed in the United States of America on acid-free paper
16 15 14 13   ML   3 4 5 6

"If the new grammar is to be brought to bear on composition, it must be brought to bear on the rhetoric of the sentence. . . . With hundreds of handbooks and rhetorics to draw from I have never been able to work out a program for teaching the sentence as I find it in the work of contemporary writers."
—Francis Christensen, "A Generative Rhetoric of the Sentence"

****

To the memory of Francis Christensen, the first to see the light: Christensen's life's work made possible this "program for teaching the sentence as [it is found] in the work of contemporary writers." We are deeply grateful to him, our silent partner, for helping us work out the program found in the sentence-composing approach.
—Don and Jenny Killgallon

Contents

A merging of grammar, composition, and literature, the sentence-composing approach uses authors as mentors in an apprenticeship in sentence carpentry. Through that approach, you will learn the grammatical tools authors use to build their sentences. Here, you'll learn more.

The most important part of sentences isn't the subject, isn't the predicate. It's the additions, the sentence parts that add more information about the subject, the predicate, or both. Here, you'll see why.

A widespread learning method, imitation helps you build better sentences through analyzing then imitating model sentences by authors. Here, you'll study how.

THE SENTENCE-COMPOSING TOOLBOX

"Good writing is about making good choices when it comes to picking the tools you plan to work with."
Stephen King, *On Writing*

NOUN GROUP: THE NAMING TOOLS

Nouns name someone or something. Noun tools enhance writing by providing detail and elaboration.

Contents

Contents

REVIEWING THE SENTENCE-COMPOSING TOOLBOX   195

This activity reviews all the sentence-composing tools and emphasizes two features of many well-built sentences: two or more of the same or different tools within a sentence.

ADDITIONS: TOOLS FOR BETTER WRITING   223

Perhaps now you know that grammar is easy and good and useful for building better sentences—and better writing. Now put the sentence-composing tools to work in a longer paper (750–1,000 words).

"Grammar is a piano I play by ear:
all I know about grammar is its power."
—Joan Didion, writer

Acknowledgments

We thank the hundreds of authors—mentors in this apprenticeship in sentence composing—whose model sentences transform literature into a legacy of lessons, providing for students voices of enduring value, voices that will help them discover their own.

A Merger of Grammar, Composition, and Literature

Grammar is easy. Grammar is good. Even though those sentences are stylistically anemic, they are the most important sentences in this book. Keep them in mind. If you think—perhaps because of negative associations in your earlier schooling— that grammar is useless and hard, substitute those two little sentences. Then, through the varied practices in this worktext using grammatical tools, you will learn to build better sentences than you've ever written, built like those of authors. Grammar, then, is useful.

> *"English grammar is so interesting because it is so simple."*
> —Gertrude Stein, avant-garde author

Although grammar is easy and good, writing is good, but isn't easy. How can something easy, like grammar, make something difficult, like writing, easier?

> *"Writing is easy: All you do is sit staring at a blank sheet of paper*
> *[or a blank screen] until drops of blood form on your forehead."*
> —Gene Fowler, writer

Since writing unfolds one sentence at a time, learning to build better sentences—the goal of *Grammar for College Writing: A Sentence-Composing Approach*— makes writing easier. It does so by giving you mentors in sentence composing, authors like Stephen King, J. K. Rowling, Ernest Hemingway, Toni Morrison, Ian McEwan, Jhumpa Lahiri, Barack Obama, James Joyce, Mitch Albom, Stephenie Meyers, John Steinbeck, Ray Bradbury, and hundreds more who serve as your mentors in your apprenticeship in building better sentences. Their sentences, the basis for all the practices in this worktext, reveal the tools they use to build those sentences. The practices in this worktext teach those tools. Through literary sentences as models for grammatical tools, you will learn the sentence in the story, and the story in the sentence, linking grammar, composition, and literature.

Zooming in on literary sentences in your reading creates a user's guide to sentence carpentry for building better sentences.

> *"Jack Kerouac probably learned how to construct his astonishing*
> *sentences through his extensive reading: he haunted the local library,*
> *gobbling down everything he could get his hands on."*
> —Kitty Burns Florey, *Sister Bernadette's Barking Dog*

The heart of this worktext, the sentence-composing toolbox, contains tools used frequently by authors, infrequently by many students—grammatical structures easy to learn, practice, and use to build better sentences through the sentence-composing approach used in thousands of classrooms, from elementary school through college. That approach uses, systematically and exclusively, model sentences by authors for practices in building better sentences.

It works mainly through imitation. Think about how you learned to pitch a baseball, sew a button, do the latest dance, style your hair, tie a tie, shave your face, make a bed, or almost anything. Probably someone demonstrated how to do it. In this worktext, authors demonstrate how you can build better sentences by using the same tools they do.

Most authors learned to write through reading and imitating, at least to a certain extent. You'll go through a similar process in the practices in this worktext.

"It is by imitation, far more than by precept, that we learn everything."
—Edmund Burke, author

Imitating examines authors' sentences under a microscope, where you can see, clearly and easily, their parts, arrangements, and relationships to each other. Through imitation, that magnification is an enormous help in demonstrating that good sentences are composed carefully, not written spontaneously. Good writers don't write the way they speak, or speak the way they write. Good writers build sentences; they don't say them.

"I am sick to death of the wide gap of embarrassing differences between my writing and speaking voices!"
—J. D. Salinger, "Hapworth 16, 1924"

You'll begin your apprenticeship in building better sentences by first learning how to imitate sentences of authors, and then opening the sentence-composing toolbox to learn the tools authors use to build their sentences.

Writing unfolds one sentence at a time. Sentences unfold one part at a time. Good sentences are the result of good sentence parts. Good sentence parts are the result of sentence-composing tools like the ones authors use, those in this worktext, an indispensable collection for mastering sentence carpentry.

"Read, read, read. Read everything, and see how they do it. Just like a carpenter who works as an apprentice and studies the master. Read! You'll absorb it. Then write."
—William Faulkner, novelist

Learning, practicing, and especially using the tools of sentence carpentry are the purposes of *Grammar for College Writing: A Sentence-Composing Approach*. Study how the master carpenters—the hundreds of authors in this worktext—use those tools. Fill your toolbox with their tools. Then write.

How many sentence parts do sentences need? Sentences need two: a subject and a predicate. How many sentence parts do almost all sentences have? Sentences have three, a subject, predicate, *and additions*.

As almost everyone realizes, the two required parts are a subject and a predicate. Not much to say there. A subject is the topic of the sentence, and a predicate is a comment about that topic.

As almost no one realizes, those two parts are almost never the most important. The most important parts are the additions, which are the sentence parts that carry most of the sentence's meaning, providing more information about the subject, the predicate, or both. Because additions generate sentence power through elaboration, most authors' sentences but relatively few students' sentences contain them. This worktext aims at bridging that gap by zooming in on those additions, which are the sentence parts that expand, amplify, deepen the meaning within a sentence. Additions are the tools that all skillful writers use to build their sentences. Those tools are the focus of this worktext, *Grammar for College Writing: A Sentence-Composing Approach*.

Contrast the pairs of sentences below. In each pair, the first sentence has just two sentence parts: subject and predicate. The second sentence in each pair, the original sentence by J. K. Rowling, author of the Harry Potter series, uses additions (in boldface) for elaboration. Think of subjects and predicates as just the frame for a picture, and think of the additions, far more important than the frame, as the picture.

SUBJECT AND PREDICATE	**ADDITIONS**
Dudley turned to Harry. J. K. Rowling, *Harry Potter and the Chamber of Secrets*	Dudley, **who was so large his bottom drooped over either side of the kitchen chair**, turned to Harry.
The troll was advancing on her. J. K. Rowling, *Harry Potter and the Sorcerer's Stone*	The troll was advancing on her, **knocking the sinks off the wall as it went.**
Then they visited the Apothecary. J.K. Rowling, *Harry Potter and the Sorcerer's Stone*	Then they visited the Apothecary, **which was fascinating enough to make up for its horrible smell, a mixture of bad eggs and rotted cabbages.**

They studied Red Caps.

> J. K. Rowling, *Harry Potter and the Prisoner of Azkaban*

They studied Red Caps, **the nasty little goblinlike creatures that lurked wherever there had been bloodshed, in the dungeons of castles, in the potholes of deserted battlefields, waiting to bludgeon those who had gotten lost.**

Harry sat motionless in his chair.

> J. K. Rowling, *Harry Potter and the Chamber of Secrets*

Harry sat motionless in his chair, **stunned by the serpent's stare.**

She flicked her wand.

> J. K. Rowling, *Harry Potter and the Chamber of Secrets*

She flicked her wand, **casually, at the dishes in the sink, which began to clean themselves, clinking gently in the background.**

The snake slithered.

> J. K. Rowling, *Harry Potter and the Chamber of Secrets*

Enraged, hissing furiously, the snake slithered **straight toward Justin Finch-Fletchley, its fangs exposed, poised to strike.**

The snake raised its head.

> J. K. Rowling, *Harry Potter and the Sorcerer's Stone*

Slowly, very slowly, the snake raised its head **until its eyes were on a level with Harry's.**

Neville hobbled off with Madame Hooch.

> J. K. Rowling, *Harry Potter and the Sorcerer's Stone*

His face tear-streaked, clutching his wrist, Neville hobbled off with Madame Hooch, **who had her arm around him.**

Harry watched.

> J. K. Rowling, *Harry Potter and the Chamber of Secrets*

Harry watched, **amazed, as a portly ghost approached the table, crouched low, and walked through it, his mouth held wide so that it passed through one of the stinking salmon.**

Professor Dumbledore was standing by the mantelpiece.

> J. K. Rowling, *Harry Potter and the Chamber of Secrets*

Professor Dumbledore was standing by the mantelpiece, **beaming, near Professor McGonagall, who was taking great gasps, clutching her chest.**

He got to his feet.

> J. K. Rowling, *Harry Potter and the Chamber of Secrets*

Dizzy, covered in soot, he got to his feet, **gingerly, holding his broken glasses up to his eyes.**

Dobby stood.

> J. K. Rowling, *Harry Potter and the Chamber of Secrets*

Cowering behind, his legs wrapped heavily in bandages, Dobby stood.

Snape smirked.

> J. K. Rowling, *Harry Potter and the Chamber of Secrets*

Snape smirked **as he swept off around the dungeon, not spotting Seamus Finnigan, who was pretending to vomit into his cauldron.**

Clearly, the additions, not the subjects and predicates, create well-built sentences. J. K. Rowling, the author of the sentences, whose Harry Potter series has sold over 400 million books so far, would not have made publishing history with just subjects and predicates. With only them and nothing else, J. K. Rowling would have sold none of her books. With subjects, predicates, *and additions*, the books made history.

Forget subjects and predicates. Emphasize tools instead—for additions, for building better sentences through elaboration—sentences like those of J. K. Rowling and, in the next activity and throughout the rest of this worktext, many other authors.

"Composition is essentially a process of <u>addition</u>."
—Francis Christensen, the pioneering linguist whose work kindled the sentence-composing approach

---

The following activity emphasizes two qualities of well-written sentences. The first is **additions**, which means *inserting sentence parts for elaboration and variety*. The second is **positions**, which means *varying the places within the sentence where those additions occur.*

Directions: Below are thirty stripped-down sentences, minus additions. Put the additions back into the sentences, in any effective positions. Then, a second time, put them back into different places. Use commas where needed.

Example:

The grass was high.

a. around the old gravestones
b. unattended

E. L. Doctorow, *The Waterworks*

Two Acceptable Arrangements:

1a. Around the gravestones, the grass, unattended, was high.

1b. Unattended, the grass around the gravestones was high.

(*Other acceptable arrangements are possible.*)

---

1. I awoke.
   a. feeling able to talk to him
   b. finally

   Octavia E. Butler, *Kindred*

2. Gramps had been thrown out of high school for misbehavior.
   a. punching the principal in the nose
   b. by the age of fifteen

   Barack Obama, *Dreams from My Father*

3. You know that you read.
   a. actively
   b. when you've finished reading a book
   c. if the pages are filled with your notes

   Mortimer Adler, "How to Mark a Book"

4. Sandy Glass smiled most.
   a. brimming with the irrepressible joy of his own intelligence
   b. cheerful
   c. when he was angry

   Allegra Goodman, *Intuition*

5. Burnham demanded.
   a. that the steward return to the wireless room for an explanation
   b. footsore and irritable

   > Eric Larson, *The Devil in the White City*

6. He rolled up his shirt and placed it under his head.
   a. tilting it just enough for the rain to flow down about his face
   b. to keep the rain out of his nose

   > Edward P. Jones, *The Known World*

7. The girls hovered around her.
   a. after their father's death
   b. watched everything she did, followed her through the house

   > Marilynne Robinson, *Housekeeping*

8. Joy leapt in his father's heart for his son.
   a. thirsty for knowledge
   b. who was quick to learn

   > Hermann Hesse, *Siddhartha*

9. He liked shooting things.
   a. and wrestling with his father
   b. hammering things, smashing things

   > Jeffrey Eugenides, *Middlesex*

10. They stood.
    a. in the gathering shadows
    b. in front of the barracks
    c. while their American friend came forward

    > Tracy Kidder, *Mountains Beyond Mountains*

11. They stood in the dead city
    a. a heap of boys
    b. daring each other in shrieky whispers
    c. their hiking lunches half devoured

    > Ray Bradbury, *The Martian Chronicles*

12. Her father carried the water.
    a. through the kitchen door outside
    b. slowly and carefully
    c. taking oddly small steps

    Jhumpa Lahiri, *Unaccustomed Earth*

13. Maier Christian sat.
    a. and examined his forest plan
    b. on a log in the sun
    c. his boots half-buried in slushy snow

    Perri Knize, *A Piano Odyssey*

14. The voice that answered had an Indian lilt to its Canadian accent.
    a. unmistakable
    b. like a trace of incense in the air
    c. light

    Yann Martel, *Life of Pi*

15. To the left was a doorway.
    a. where twenty ranch hands used to eat dinner in the hot summer nights of harvest
    b. off the kitchen
    c. and lay the screened porch

    Joyce Weatherford, *Heart of the Beast*

16. Below the pulpit sat the congregation, and lay the casket.
    a. pearly gray
    b. stood the minister
    c. decorated with a spray of white flowers

    Anne Tyler, *Saint Maybe*

17. Sarah kissed Mack on the forehead.
    a. and then held on to Nan when she again broke into sobs and moans
    b. simply
    c. tears rolling down her cheeks

    William P. Young, *The Shack*

18. Josef took him into his arms, and thought suddenly how long it had been.
    a. a sound that had once been as common in the house as the teakettle whistle
    b. since he had heard the sound of Thomas freely crying
    c. stiffly

    Michael Chabon, *The Amazing Adventures of Kavalier & Clay*

19. I crept over to the bedroll.
    a. which was battered both front and back
    b. and tried to find a comfortable place for my head
    c. when Walter finished cleaning my cuts and removing glass from my hair

    Sara Gruen, *Water for Elephants*

20. We laughed, too.
    a. to make him happy
    b. which were rusty way before I had him
    c. when our teacher laughed at his own jokes
    d. forcing it sometimes

    Alice Sebold, *The Lovely Bones*

21. Indian Ed climbed.
    a. where the team had spent the night with their cache of stolen goods
    b. two pack animals and a half dozen horses
    c. in a side canyon, on a late February morning
    d. across the rocks below the overhang

    Aron Ralston, *Between a Rock and a Hard Place*

22. Each tooth was still there.
    a. intact
    b. later
    c. when he found the courage to check with his fingers
    d. to his relief

    Markus Zusak, *The Book Thief*

23. She came to greet him.
    a. kissing him on the cheek
    b. barefoot

    c. embracing him

    d. holding her arms wide

J. M. Coetzee, Disgrace

24. I rode my bicycle to the delivery point.

    a. where Eugene Haverford used to sit in the darkness talking about the news of the day

    b. at five the next morning

    c. with skill and swiftness

    d. as I folded newspapers

Pat Conroy, South of Broad

25. A baseball is made of a composition-cork nucleus.

    a. which is held together with 216 slightly raised red cotton stitches

    b. encased in two thin layers of rubber

    c. surrounded by 12 yards of tightly wrapped blue-gray wool yarn, 45 yards of white wool yarn, 54 more yards of blue-gray wool yarn, 150 yards of fine cotton yarn, a coat of rubber cement, and a cowhide (formerly horse-hide) exterior

    d. one black and one red

Roger Angell, Five Seasons

26. There he stood.

    a. beaming at his discovery, sharing it with me

    b. the most recent eructation (belching) of the ruling corporate elite

    c. without thinking or even dreaming for a moment that I might actually understand what he was referring to

    d. a class that reproduces itself solely by means of virtuous and proper hiccups

Muriel Barbery, The Elegance of the Hedgehog

27. There was no foundry, no vehicle company, or no manufacturer.

    a. to make a locomotive or a gun or powder

    b. in early California

    c. to make iron products like railroad tracks

    d. to make carriages horse-drawn or for a train

Stephen E. Ambrose, Nothing Like It in the World

28. The dog's valor had one flaw.
    a. because if the intruders were armed, his head dropped, his tail turned in
    b. alert
    c. although he was a good sentry
    d. ever ready to raise Cain

    Truman Capote, *In Cold Blood*

29. The garden vegetation rose up.
    a. whose steady motion of advance and withdrawal made sounds of gentle thunder, then sudden hissing against the pebbles
    b. sensuous
    c. and tropical in its profusion
    d. an effect heightened by the gray, soft light and a delicate mist drifting in from the sea

    Ian McEwan, *On Chesil Beach*

30. Claude lay in the middle of the messy barn.
    a. fingers half curled beside a liquor bottle
    b. on a hastily improvised bed of straw bales
    c. palm up
    d. one hand hanging slackly to the floor

    David Wroblewski, *The Story of Edgar Sawtelle*

Contrast the Dick-and-Jane sentences below with the originals. By contrast, the originals are filled with sentence-composing tools that add meaning, texture, style, variety, and elaboration. *Additions and positions of tools make all the difference in composing well-written sentences.*

Sentences Minus Tools:

1. I awoke.

2. Gramps had been thrown out of high school for misbehavior.

3. You know that you read.

4. Sandy Glass smiled most.

5. Burnham demanded.

6. He rolled up his shirt and placed it under his head.

7. The girls hovered around her.

8. Joy leapt in his father's heart for his son.

9. He liked shooting things.

10. They stood.

11. They stood in the dead city.

12. Her father carried the water

13. Maier Christian sat.

14. The voice that answered had an Indian lilt to its Canadian accent.

15. To the left was a doorway.

16. Below the pulpit sat the congregation, and lay the casket.

17. Sarah kissed Mack on the forehead.

18. Josef took him into his arms, and thought suddenly how long it had been.

19. I crept over to the bedroll.

20. We laughed, too.

21. Indian Ed climbed across the rocks below the overhang.

22. Each tooth was still there.

23. She came to greet him.

24. I rode my bicycle to the delivery point.

25. A baseball is made of a composition-cork nucleus.

26. There he stood.

27. There was no foundry, no vehicle company, or no manufacturer.

28. The dog's valor had one flaw.

29. The garden vegetation rose up.

30. Claude lay in the middle of the messy barn.

After learning in the next section how to imitate sentences by authors, you will in the rest of this worktext learn, practice, and use all of the sentence-composing tools from the activity on additions and positions. Throughout *Grammar for College Writing: A Sentence-Composing Approach*, with authors as master craftsmen for your mentors, you'll learn the tools they use for sentence carpentry. With those tools, you'll be able to build better sentences.

"There is a kind of carpentry in sentence-making, various ways of joining or hooking up modifying units to the base sentence that preserve us from the tedium of Dick-and-Jane sentences."
—Mina P. Shaughnessy, *Errors and Expectations*

Imitation: A Step to Creation

You now know that it's not the subject and predicate that make good sentences. It's the additions.

You can learn the tools authors use for additions. A good way to begin is to imitate the way authors use those tools to build their sentences. What follows are practices in sentence imitating.

After you learn how to imitate sentences, throughout the rest of this worktext you'll use sentence imitating and other methods to learn grammatical tools hundreds of authors use to build their sentences. All of those tools develop the most important part of any sentence: *the additions.*

CHUNKING TO IMITATE

In these activities, based on sentences by J. K. Rowling from the Harry Potter series of novels, you will become aware of meaningful divisions within sentences, an awareness you'll need to imitate model sentences. You will learn that authors compose their sentences one "chunk" or meaningful sentence part at a time.

Directions (Part One): Copy the sentence divided into meaningful chunks.

1a. Dudley, who was so large his / bottom drooped over either side of the kitchen / chair, turned to Harry.

1b. Dudley, / who was so large his bottom drooped over either side of the kitchen chair, / turned to Harry.

J. K. Rowling, Harry Potter and the Chamber of Secrets

2a. The troll was advancing on her, / knocking the sinks off the wall / as it went.

2b. The troll was / advancing on her, knocking the / sinks off the wall as it went.

J. K. Rowling, Harry Potter and the Sorcerer's Stone

3a. Then they visited the Apothecary, which / was fascinating enough to make up for its / horrible smell, a mixture of bad / eggs and rotted cabbages.

3b. Then they visited the Apothecary, / which was fascinating enough / to make up for its horrible smell, / a mixture of bad eggs and rotted cabbages.

J. K. Rowling, Harry Potter and the Sorcerer's Stone

Directions (Part Two): Copy the model and then copy the sentence that can be divided into chunks that match the chunks in the model.

1. MODEL: Enraged, hissing furiously, the snake slithered straight toward Justin Finch-Fletchley, its fangs exposed, poised to strike.

   J. K. Rowling, *Harry Potter and the Chamber of Secrets*

   a. Near the ladder, the open paint can presented a hazard, with small children on the playground in jeopardy.
   b Frightened, hiding nervously, the rabbit burrowed backward in the bush, its eyes blinking, ready to bolt.

2. MODEL: She flicked her wand, casually, at the dishes in the sink, which began to clean themselves, clinking gently in the background.

   J. K. Rowling, *Harry Potter and the Chamber of Secrets*

   a. Juan nodded his head, slowly, at the toddler in the corner, who started to approach him, smiling confidently on the way.
   b. All of a sudden, the moon turned green on the horizon, an amazing phenomenon that went unexplained by scientists.

3. MODEL: They studied Red Caps, the nasty little goblinlike creatures that lurked wherever there had been bloodshed, in the dungeons of castles, in the potholes of deserted battlefields, waiting to bludgeon those who had gotten lost.

   J. K. Rowling, *Harry Potter and the Prisoner of Azkaban*

   a. In the course, we studied sentence structure, analyzing the sentences of master authors, whose sentences served as models for us to imitate, a process that was the beginning of our quest for mastery of sentence variety.
   b. Cranston sought special spiders, the stealthy bulbous vampirelike species that lived wherever they could weave webs, in the high eaves of barns, in the bushes of nearby bogs, hoping to capture flies that had grown fat.

Directions (Part Three): Copy the model and then copy the sentence that imitates it. Then chunk both into meaningful sentence parts, using slash marks (/).

1. MODEL: Slowly, very slowly, the snake raised its head until its eyes were on a level with Harry's.

   J. K. Rowling, *Harry Potter and the Sorcerer's Stone*

a. Tense, very tense, Alfredo approached his boss, someone he always considered a sarcastic, unpleasant curmudgeon.

b. Quietly, very quietly, Bridgette crossed the room until her hands were on the diary of her sister.

2. MODEL: His face tear-streaked, clutching his wrist, Neville hobbled off with Madame Hooch, who had her arm around him.

J. K. Rowling, *Harry Potter and the Sorcerer's Stone*

a. Her performance over, holding the trophy, Kelly walked into the wings toward her mom, who extended her arms in congratulations.

b. A new wireless vehicle, that invention was a techno-gadget unequalled by the competition because it could teleport its owner anywhere.

3. MODEL: Harry watched, amazed, as a portly ghost approached the table, crouched low, and walked through it, his mouth held wide so that it passed through one of the stinking salmon.

J. K. Rowling, *Harry Potter and the Chamber of Secrets*

a. Samantha listened, astonished, as a younger player raised her violin, concentrated deeply, and played through the piece, her bow moving perfectly so that she perfected each note of the demanding concerto.

b. His right pant leg torn from catching on the nail, Jameson inspected the tear, considered mending it himself but decided instead to ask his mom, who would kid him about his lack of sewing skill.

IMITATING MODEL SENTENCES

In the following activities here and throughout the worktext, you'll build your sentences like those by authors through imitating their sentence structure but using your own content. Before beginning each imitation, first think of interesting content—maybe a situation or character from a book, movie, TV show, or news event—or use your imagination to create original content.

Directions (Part Four): Match the model and its imitation. Copy both sentences. Then chunk both, using a slash (/) between sentence parts. Finally, write your own imitation of each model.

Imitation: A Step to Creation

1. MODEL: Professor Dumbledore was standing by the mantelpiece, beaming, near Professor McGonagall, who was taking great gasps, clutching her chest.

   J. K. Rowling, *Harry Potter and the Chamber of Secrets*

Imitations:

   a. The parent was looking down the table, smiling, beside the host, who was showing unvarnished pride, describing the recipe.
   b. Once in a while, when time hung heavy, I would take a walk in the woods not far from my house, listening to nature's music.

2. MODEL: Dizzy, covered in soot, he got to his feet, gingerly, holding his broken glasses up to his eyes.

   J. K. Rowling, *Harry Potter and the Chamber of Secrets*

Imitations:

   a. Alone, alarmed by noises, he walked down the stairs, quietly, hearing some strangers' voices in the next room.
   b. In twilight, before the new moon, the romance began, a strange relationship that confused but enthralled her.

3. MODEL: Cowering behind, his legs wrapped heavily in bandages, Dobby stood.

   J. K. Rowling, *Harry Potter and the Chamber of Secrets*

Imitations:

   a. Running at his fastest pace, nearing the finish line, he dodged a little kid.
   b. Standing nearby, his patient covered lightly in blankets, the surgeon waited.

Directions (Part Five): Study the models and sample imitations, and then write an imitation of each model sentence so good that nobody can tell your sentence from the J. K. Rowling's sentence.

1. MODEL: As they drew nearer to the silhouetted figure at the table, Voldemort's face shone through the gloom, hairless, snakelike, with slits for nostrils and gleaming red eyes, whose pupils were vertical.

   J. K. Rowling, *Harry Potter and the Deathly Hallows*

Sample: While the kids approached closer to the pacing tiger in its cage, the trainer's voice barked suddenly at the audience, loud, clear, with cautions about safety and threats to the children, whose parents were nearby.

2. MODEL: Harry leaned forward to see Hagrid, who was ruby-red in the face and staring down at his enormous hands, his wide grin hidden in the tangle of his black beard.

> J. K. Rowling, *Harry Potter and the Prisoner of Azkaban*

Sample: The coach looked over to calm the player's little brother, who was very upset at the catcher and glaring at the umpire on the mound, his angry eyes flashing in the triangle of his little face.

3. MODEL: Harry twisted his body around and saw a grindylow, a small, horned water demon, poking out of the weed, its long fingers clutched tightly around Harry's leg, its pointed fangs bared.

> J. K. Rowling, *Harry Potter and the Goblet of Fire*

Sample: Frank plumbed his thoughts thoroughly and got an idea, an amazing, little devious strategy, popping out of his mind, its emerging details flowing easily from his brain, its salient points brilliant.

"Imitation precedes creation."
—Stephen King, *On Writing*

Previewing the Noun Tools

Nouns <u>name</u>. This section introduces you to the noun group of sentence-composing tools: words, phrases, and clauses that *name* someone or something.

After this introduction, you'll focus on the particular naming tools in the noun group, learn about each tool in depth, practice using the tool through varied activities, and apply the tool in a piece of your writing.

NOUN WORDS	NOUN PHRASES	NOUN CLAUSES
Basketball is fun.	**Playing basketball** is fun. or **To play basketball** is fun. or The best sport, **the game of basketball**, is fun.	**How I play basketball** is fun. or Fun is **why I play basketball**. or **That I play basketball** is fun.

SENTENCES FROM CHILDREN'S LITERATURE
"There are perhaps no days of our childhood we lived so
fully as those we spent with a favorite book."
—Marcel Proust, author

In the rest of this section, you'll study noun tools—*the tools that name*—in sentences from famous children's literature, stories like *A Wrinkle in Time, Holes, Bridge to Terabithia, How to Eat Fried Worms, The Chronicles of Narnia,* and others. Their authors, like writers of literature for any age group—children, adolescents, or adults—use noun tools to add detail, variety, maturity, and sophistication to their sentences. Study, imitate, and learn from their sentences while taking a memory trip down childhood's Literary Lane.

Noun Phrases: There are three kinds of noun phrases: gerund, infinitive, appositive. All of them *name* someone or something.

1. **Gerund Phrase**—Begins with an *ing* word: *searching for lost coins, memorizing new poems, climbing mountains.*

Examples:

<u>Being bitten by a scorpion or even a rattlesnake</u> is not the worst thing that can happen to you. *(Names what isn't the worst thing that can happen.)*

> Louis Sachar, *Holes*

Harry was a white dog with black spots who liked everything except <u>getting a bath</u>. *(Names the exception.)*

> Gene Zion, "Harry the Dirty Dog"

The velveteen rabbit grew to like <u>sleeping in the boy's bed</u>, for the boy made nice tunnels for him under the bedclothes that he said were like the burrows the real rabbits lived in. *(Names what the rabbit grew to like.)*

> Margery Williams, *The Velveteen Rabbit*

---

2. **Infinitive Phrase**—Begins with the word *to* plus a verb: *<u>to study</u> bugs, <u>to get</u> a new haircut, <u>to take</u> a computer apart.*

Examples:

<u>To get Janice Avery without ending up squashed or suspended</u> was their problem. *(Names their problem.)*

> Katherine Paterson, *Bridge to Terabithia*

Now Tom began <u>to scrawl something on the slate</u>, hiding the words from the girl. *(Names what Tom began to do.)*

> Mark Twain, *The Adventures of Tom Sawyer*

Violet turned on a light and began <u>to sketch out her idea on a pad of paper</u>. *(Names what Violet began to do.)*

> Lemony Snicket, *A Series of Unfortunate Events: The End*

---

3. **Appositive Phrase**—Usually begins with one of these words—*a, an, the*—and identifies something named elsewhere in the sentence, often next to the appositive phrase.

Examples:

Bess led the way around the house to the spring house, <u>a windowless adobe structure built onto the back wall of the kitchen</u>. *(Names what the spring house was.)*

> Carolyn Keene, Nancy Drew series, *The Secret of Shadow Ranch*

After they had licked their paws and whiskers, Butterfly, <u>the lovely Persian cat</u>, brought out her nose flute and began to play. *(Names what Butterfly was.)*

Esther Averill, *Jenny and the Cat Club*

Brigitte could see what a sad and abandoned child Lucky was, <u>an orphan whose Guardian was too busy for hugging</u>. *(Names who Lucky was.)*

Susan Patron, *The Higher Power of Lucky*

Noun Clauses: Usually begin with one of these words—*what, how, that, why*. They are sentence parts (<u>not</u> complete sentences) containing a subject (underlined <u>once</u>) and a predicate (underlined <u>twice</u>).

what <u>humidity</u> <u><u>measures</u></u>	***that*** <u>math</u> <u><u>began long ago</u></u>
what <u>Mars</u> <u><u>is like</u></u>	***that*** <u>pizza</u> <u><u>is American</u></u>
how <u>the earth</u> <u><u>formed</u></u>	***why*** <u>people</u> <u><u>enjoy dessert</u></u>
how <u>a baby</u> <u><u>laughs</u></u>	***why*** <u>dogs</u> <u><u>bark</u></u>

Examples:

Prince Caspian knew <u>that he had done a terrible thing</u>. *(Names what Prince Caspian knew.)*

C. S. Lewis, *The Chronicles of Narnia*

Harry the dog fell asleep in his favorite place, happily dreaming about <u>how he thoroughly enjoyed getting dirty.</u> *(Names what Harry the dog was dreaming about.)*

Gene Zion, "Harry the Dirty Dog"

No grown-up will ever understand <u>that this is a matter of so much importance</u>! *(Names what grown-ups don't understand.)*

Antoine de Saint Exupéry, *The Little Prince*

I still understood <u>why I had always hated Lucinda's gift</u>. *(Names what was still understood.)*

Gail Carson Levine, *Ella Enchanted*

Review

Directions: For sentences with **boldfaced** noun tools, exchange one of your own for the author's. For sentences with _deleted_ noun tools, expand the sentence by adding one of your own at the caret (^).

EXAMPLE OF EXCHANGING ———————————————

Author's: **Pushing the handcart up to the man's house** was difficult.

> John Hersey, _Hiroshima_

Yours: **Carrying our sick sheepdog into the vet's office** was difficult.

EXAMPLE OF EXPANDING ————————————————

Author's Sentence with Deleted Tool: Arranging ^ can give a sense of quiet in a crowded day, like writing a poem, or saying a prayer.

Your Added Tool: **Arranging a schedule without lots of activities** can give a sense of quiet in a crowded day, like writing a poem, or saying a prayer.

Original Sentence: **Arranging a bowl of flowers in the morning** can give a sense of quiet in a crowded day, like writing a poem, or saying a prayer.

> Anne Morrow Lindbergh, _Gift from the Sea_

Noun Phrases: Exchange the first five. Expand the next five.

1. They all saw the strange creature, **a whiskered furry face that looked out at them from behind a tree.**

   > C. S. Lewis, _The Chronicles of Narnia_

2. Mrs. Myers tried **to figure out where to put the extra desk.**

   > Katherine Paterson, _Bridge to Terabithia_

3. He started **waking up before the alarm that week,** fresher in the morning and stronger.

   > Robert Lipsyte, _The Contender_

4. She periodically tried **to dress the cat in doll clothes** and **to make it sit at picnics.**

   > Gary Paulsen, _The Time Hackers_

5. Maybe their father would bring presents, **a package of colored paper for Ramona, a paperback book for Beezus.**

    Beverly Cleary, *Ramona and Her Father*

6. Being a ^ doesn't excuse you from having to learn.

    Bill and Vera Cleaver, *Where the Lilies Bloom*

7. May always liked the weird ones best, the ones ^.

    Cynthia Rylant, *Missing May*

8. He preferred visiting ^ and listening ^.

    Louis Sachar, *Holes*

9. Most of the natives Tommy knew did their shopping on King Street, the ^ , a ^ .

    Tracy Kidder, *Home Town*

10. On this planet everything is in perfect order because everybody has learned to ^, to ^, to ^.

    Madeleine L'Engle, *A Wrinkle in Time*

Noun Clauses: Exchange the first five. Expand the next five.

11. **What Jim Thatcher had said about her man** could have been a trick.

    Hal Borland, *When the Legends Die*

12. Up until I turned twelve years old, the kind of friends I had were **what you'd expect.**

    Joseph Krumgold, *Onion John*

13. Mr. Monroe sat down in a daze as if he were wondering **how he came to be sitting in his own living room in a wet raincoat with a strange bunny on his lap.**

    Deborah and James Howe, *Bunnicula*

14. Agnes had long red hair that fell rather greasily to her waist, and when she sidled up to Gilly on the playground, the first thing Gilly noticed was **how dirty her fingernails were.**

    Katherine Paterson, *The Great Gilly Hopkins*

15. His parents concluded **that something dreadful must have happened** and **that they would probably never see their son again**.

> William Steig, "Sylvester and the Magic Pebble"

16. Because of the routines we follow, we often forget that ^ .

> Maya Angelou, *Wouldn't Take Nothing for My Journey Now*

17. What ^ was a box in one corner of the room, a box with dials and a small light shining on the front.

> Robert C. O'Brien, *Mrs. Frisby and the Rats of NIMH*

18. The three children did not understand how ^, or how ^.

> Lemony Snicket, *A Series of Unfortunate Events: The End*

19. I asked him once why ^, why ^.

> Mildred D. Taylor, *Roll of Thunder, Hear My Cry*

20. There was a terrible moment when Father insisted that ^, that ^, and that ^.

> Kate DiCamillo, *The Miraculous Journey of Edward Tulane*

"When I said, 'A rose is a rose is a rose is a rose,'
I completely caressed and addressed a noun."
—Gertrude Stein, avant-garde writer

In the next pages, you'll learn and practice how authors use each of the tools in the noun group to build their sentences, and how you can use them, too.

Appositive Phrase

In each pair, the second sentence has an appositive phrase. Notice how it adds detail, elaboration, and style.

1a. He had an aunt in Winesburg, and with her he lived until she died.

1b. He had an aunt in Winesburg, **a black-toothed old woman who raised chickens**, and with her he lived until she died. (*Appositive phrase identifies* <u>*a person*</u>.)

> Sherwood Anderson, *Winesburg, Ohio*

2a. I walked along Gilman Street.

2b. I walked along Gilman Street, **the best street in town**. (*Appositive phrase identifies* <u>*a place*</u>.)

> John Knowles, *A Separate Peace*

3a. The furniture included a walnut bed whose ornate headboard rose halfway up the wall toward the high ceiling.

3b. The furniture, **a mixture of Logan crafted walnut and oak**, included a walnut bed whose ornate headboard rose halfway up the wall toward the high ceiling. (*Appositive phrase identifies* <u>*a thing*</u>.)

> Mildred D. Taylor, *Roll of Thunder, Hear My Cry*

WHAT IS AN APPOSITIVE PHRASE? *It's a noun phrase identifying a person, place, or thing already named in a sentence.* Appositives often begin with the words *a, an,* or *the.* They always answer one of these questions: Who is he? Who is she? Who are they? *(people)* What is it? What are they? *(places or things)*

Number: Sentences can contain either single or multiple appositive phrases:

Single—**A bald slight man**, he reminded me of a baby bird.

> Tracy Chevalier, *The Girl with a Pearl Earring*

Multiple—Most of the town's natives did their shopping on King Street, **the town's shopping strip, a slice of chain department stores, auto dealerships, fast-food restaurants**.

> Tracy Kidder, *Home Town*

Position: Appositive phrases occur in three positions:

Opener—**A master of disguise himself**, Yarbrough knew when he was looking at a façade.

Mary Doria Russell, *The Sparrow*

S-V split—Gas jets, **the primary source of artificial illumination**, did little to pierce Chicago's perpetual coal-smoke dusk. *(Splits the subject from the verb.)*

Eric Larson, *The Devil in the White City*

Closer—Most amusing of all was the magazine's mascot Coco, **the black human-mouse dressed in tattered poor man's robes, shawls, skullcap, and sandals**.

Roya Hakakian, *Journey from the Land of No*

PRACTICE 1: MATCHING

Match the appositive phrase with the sentence. Write out each sentence, underlining the appositive phrase.

Sentences:

1. There was no one in The Hot Spot store but Mr. Shiftlet and the boy behind the counter, ^.

   Flannery O'Connor, "The Life You Save May Be Your Own"

2. I consider my own breakfast cereal, ^ .

   Barbara Ehrenreich, *The Snarling Citizen*

3. In our clenched fists, we held our working cards from the shop, ^.

   Gerda Weissmann Klein, "All but My Life"

4. Watanabe, ^, leaned over and spoke the words in Japanese to his employer.

   Ann Patchett, *Bel Canto*

5. A gray cat, dragging its belly, crept across the lawn, and a black one, ^, trailed after.

   Katherine Mansfield, "Bliss"

Appositive Phrases:

a. a tasteless, colorless substance that clings to the stomach lining with the avidity of Krazy Glue

b. the young man who worked as Mr. Hosokawa's translator

c. its shadow

d. those sacred cards that we thought meant security

e. a pale youth with a greasy rag hung over his shoulder

PRACTICE 2: UNSCRAMBLING

Rearrange the scrambled list of sentence parts to match the structure of the model. Next, write an imitation of the model. Finally, identify the appositive phrases in the model and your imitation.

MODEL: The proprietor, a little gray man with an unkempt mustache and watery eyes, leaned on the counter, reading a newspaper.

John Steinbeck, *The Grapes of Wrath*

    a. a tall thin blonde
    b. walked down the runway
    c. with a long mane and long legs
    d. the model
    e. eyeing the audience

PRACTICE 3: COMBINING

Combine the list of sentences into just one sentence that imitates the structure of the model. Next, write an imitation of the model. Finally, identify the appositive phrases in the model and your imitation.

MODEL: A veteran bronc rider, Tom Black has ridden nine horses to death in the rodeo arena, and at every performance the spectators expect him to kill another one.

Hal Borland, *When the Legends Die*

    a. This sentence is about a fascinating historical speaker, Professor Southwick.
    b. He has visited many museums.
    c. His visits them for study of the medieval period.
    d. And at every visit the curators want him to give another lecture.

PRACTICE 4: IMITATING

Write an imitation of each model sentence that is so good that no one could guess which sentence is the author's and which is yours.

Models and Sample Imitations:

1. A golden female moth, a biggish one with a two-inch wingspread, flapped in the fire of the candle, drooped abdomen into the wet wax, stuck, flamed, and frazzled in a second.

Annie Dillard, "Death of a Moth"

Sample: A green garter snake, a skittish one with a six-inch length, slid toward the foot of the tree, parted grass in the wet yard, stopped, sensed, and disappeared in a flash.

2. The dictionary had a picture of an aardvark, a long-tailed, long-eared, burrowing African mammal living off termites caught by sticking out its tongue as an anteater does for ants.

> Malcolm X and Alex Haley, *The Autobiography of Malcolm X*

Sample: The living room contained a portrait of an ancestor, a grim-faced, black-haired disapproving matronly relative giving out disapproval signaled by looking down her nose as a parent does in disappointment.

3. A beautiful animal, it lay in the position of a marble lion, its head toward a man sitting on an upturned bucket outside the cage.

> Frank Bonham, *Chief*

Sample: A shy observer, she hesitated on the outskirts of the spirited group, her body behind a flirty girl talking with a handsome boy inside the circle.

PRACTICE 5: EXCHANGING

To practice writing good appositive phrases, exchange one of yours for the author's. Try to make yours as good as—maybe even better than—the author's.

Example:

Author's: A great many old people came and knelt around us and prayed, **the women and men with work-gnarled hands.**

> Langston Hughes, *The Big Sea*

Yours: A great many old people came and knelt around us and prayed, **the retirees and grandparents with lots of extra time.**

---

1. When the tyrannosaur roared, it was a terrifying sound, **a scream from some other world.**

> Michael Crichton, *Jurassic Park*

2. In appearance, he was the embodiment of every parent's dream, **a strong, tall, well-dressed and well-mannered boy with talent and striking looks.**

> Khaled Hosseini, *The Kite Runner*

3. Most of the town's natives did their shopping on King Street, **the town's shopping strip, a slice of chain department stores, auto dealerships, fast-food restaurants.**

Tracy Kidder, *Home Town*

PRACTICE 6: EXPANDING

Partner with the author by creating an appositive phrase at the caret (^).

1. The speech at her funeral was brief but warm about the life of Nettie Cobb, **a woman who ^, a woman who ^.**

Stephen King, *Needful Things*

2. Little Man, **a very ^ and a most ^,** was brushing his hair when I entered.

Mildred D. Taylor, *Song of the Trees*

3. **The only ^ and the weakest ^,** I was put in a special seat in the first row by the window, apart from the other children so that the teacher could tutor me without disturbing them.

Julia Alvarez, "Snow"

COMPOSITION: Technical Paper

ASSIGNMENT: Appositive phrases help readers understand unfamiliar terms because appositives define those terms. Write a five-paragraph essay about a disease, perhaps one you're already somewhat familiar with. Learn about the disease by researching your topic in the library or on the Internet. Include in your paper at least five terms unfamiliar to your readers. For each term, <u>use an appositive tool</u> to define the term so readers will clearly understand it. In addition to appositives, use other sentence-composing tools to enhance your writing.

Process:

- Introduce your essay with a paragraph that defines the disease.

- Continue with these three paragraphs:

  - how the disease is diagnosed,

  - how the disease is treated, and

  - how the results of treatment are assessed.

- Conclude with a paragraph that describes new research on the disease or predicts future treatments.

"We live in a time when the words 'impossible' and 'unsolvable' are no longer part of the scientific community's vocabulary. Each day we move closer to trials that will not just minimize the symptoms of disease and injury but eliminate them."
—Christopher Reeve, actor (played Superman in movies),
who became paralyzed, here testifying to the United States Congress

Gerund Phrase

In each pair, the second sentence has a gerund phrase. Notice how it provides detailed information.

1a. Mr. Clutter carried his apple with him when he went outdoors to examine the morning.
2a. After **drinking the glass of milk**, Mr. Clutter carried his apple with him when he went outdoors to examine the morning. *(Gerund phrase is the object of the preposition* after.*)*

> Truman Capote, *In Cold Blood*

2a. It was a ticklish job.
2b. It was a ticklish job, **saddling the pony the first time**. *(Gerund phrase is an appositive identifying "a ticklish job.")*

> Stephen King, *Needful Things*

3a. It didn't come easily, but in time he developed a skill at that.
3b. **Making new friends** didn't come easily, but in time he developed a skill at that. *(Gerund phrase is the subject that "didn't come easily.")*

> Robert Ludlum, *The Prometheus Deception*

WHAT IS A GERUND PHRASE? *It's a verbal ending in* ing *that names activities.* A verbal is a verb that also functions like another part of speech. Gerunds show action, so they act like verbs, but they also name, so they act like nouns by naming activities.

To see how gerunds function like nouns, insert any of these phrases into any of the blanks: *playing chess, learning new things, climbing mountains in distant lands, building sand castles on the beach, taking a computer apart to investigate its guts.*

1. _____ is fun. *(subject)*

2. We like _____. *(direct object)*

3. They talked about _____. *(object of preposition)*

4. A great leisure activity is _____. *(predicate noun)*

5. Their favorite pastime, _____, is enjoyed by many. *(appositive)*

Difference Between Gerunds and Present Participles—Like gerunds, present participles (page 103) are verbals that end in *ing*, but it's easy to tell the difference between them and gerunds. Present participles can be removed from the sentence without destroying the sentence, but gerunds cannot be removed without destroying the sentence. *In each pair, the first contains a present participle, and the second contains a gerund.* Notice that only the present participles can be removed.

1a. *Feeling so much better after the nap*, Gunster dressed and went out.

1b. *Feeling so much better after the nap* relieved Gunster.

2a. Ricky, *going down the staircase backward*, was very unsteady.

2b. His mom had warned Ricky about *going down the staircase backward*.

3a. The damaged plane landed poorly, *skidding left and right with sparks flying everywhere*.

3b. The captain during touchdown worried about *skidding left and right with sparks flying everywhere*.

Number: Sentences can contain either single or multiple gerund phrases:

Single—Everything necessary, books, music, wine, he could receive in any quantity by **sending a note through the window.**

Anton Chekov, "The Bet"

Multiple—My mother told me about **dressing in her best party clothes on Saturday nights** and **going to the town's plaza to promenade with her girlfriends in front of the boys they liked.**

Judith Ortiz Coffer, "The Myth of the Latin Woman"

Position: Because gerund phrases are fixed within a sentence, they cannot be moved to other positions.

Noun Group: The Naming Tools

PRACTICE 1: MATCHING

Match the gerund phrase with the sentence. Write out each sentence, underlining the gerund phrase.

Sentences:

1. I tried ^, but the twins simply watched, passive and inert as two dumb toads.
   Keith Donohue, *The Stolen Child*

2. ^ was half the battle won, for I was soon able to put the letters together and to form little words.
   Christy Brown, *My Left Foot*

3. He got a job with a storekeeper, whom he impressed by ^.
   Stephen E. Ambrose, *Nothing Like It in the World*

4. Thirty-four, balding, hawk-faced, and intense, he had been dismissed by Johns Hopkins as a graduate student, for ^.
   Michael Crichton, *Jurassic Park*

5. I started ^, a perfect one from perfectly white snow, perfectly spherical, squeezed perfectly translucent so no snow remained all the way through.
   Annie Dillard, *An American Childhood*

Gerund Phrases:

a. knowing the alphabet

b. planning gene therapy on human patients minus the proper FDS protocols

c. memorizing both the wholesale and retail cost of every item in the cluttered stock and calculating, without pencil or paper, the profit that could be expected from each piece *(Contains two gerund phrases.)*

d. making funny faces, tickling them under their fat chins, dancing like a puppet, and whistling like a mockingbird *(Contains four gerund phrases.)*

e. making an iceball

37

PRACTICE 2: UNSCRAMBLING

Rearrange the scrambled list of sentence parts to match the structure of the model. Next, write an imitation of the model. Finally, identify the gerund phrases in the model and your imitation.

MODEL: I remember the bitter fifth-grade conflict that I started by elbowing aside a bigger boy named Barry and seizing the cafeteria's last carton of chocolate milk.

Jon Katz, "How Boys Become Men"

a. and wearing the football team's championship jersey during homeroom
b. by cheering with a boisterous girl named Zee-Zee
c. that I originated
d. I recalled a zany high school custom

PRACTICE 3: COMBINING

Combine the list of sentences into just one sentence that imitates the structure of the model. Next, write an imitation of the model. Finally, identify the gerund phrases in the model and your imitation.

MODEL: Spraying bright colors, dancing, and singing are all part of the excitement.

Charles R. Joy, "Hindu Girl of Surinam"

a. Three activities are expectations of the game.
b. One is hiding borrowed objects.
c. Another is prevaricating.
d. And another is pretending.

PRACTICE 4: IMITATING

Write an imitation of each model sentence so good that nobody can tell yours from the author's.

Models and Sample Imitations:

1. Arranging a bowl of flowers in the morning can give a sense of quiet in a crowded day, like writing a poem, or saying a prayer.

Anne Morrow Lindbergh, *Gift from the Sea*

Sample: Remembering a moment of pleasure from the day will provide a source of happiness for a nice daydream, like whistling a tune, or smelling a rose.

2. Feeding our bellies seemed a more vital job to us than trying to feed our minds.

   Christy Brown, *My Left Foot*

   Sample: Sharing my mind was a more acceptable activity to her than wishing to share my heart.

3. When he got to the stump end, he steadied himself by gripping a hornlike pair of limbs and settled his sternum against a branch and lay outstretched, a swimmer among tree boughs.

   David Wroblewski, *The Story of Edgar Sawtelle*

   Sample: While she maneuvered in the deep water, she calmed herself by recalling a reassuring moment of peace and peddled her feet within the depths and worked steadily, a navigator in troubled waters.

PRACTICE 5: EXCHANGING

To practice writing good gerund phrases, exchange one of yours for the author's. Try to make yours as good as—maybe even better than—the author's.

Example:

Author's: Before **evacuating the wounded priests**, the others passed the cakes around and helped themselves.

John Hersey, *Hiroshima*

Yours: Before **finishing the sandwiches**, the others passed the cakes around and helped themselves.

1. After **scraping the wood from the shed clean**, she filled her arms with as much dry wood as she could.

   Toni Morrison, *Beloved*

2. Patty Lareine had large vices, but she also had the nice virtue of not **being a snob**.

   Norman Mailer, *Tough Guys Don't Dance*

3. Sadako's friends began to dream of **building a monument to her and all children who were killed by the atom bomb**.

   Eleanor Coerr, *Sadako and the Thousand Paper Cranes*

PRACTICE 6: EXPANDING

Partner with the author by creating a gerund phrase at the caret (^).

1. The first part of a medical student's clinical work involves ^.

   Michael Crichton, *Travels*

2. To be awake in the cool of morning on a bench near train tracks, hungry, with a little breeze blowing, and whatever book you were reading open in your lap, was a little like ^.

   David Guterson, *The Other*

3. On ^, he walked straight up to his room without ^. *(Contains two gerund phrases.)*

   Kenneth Brower, *The Starship and the Canoe*

COMPOSITION: Gerund Poem

ASSIGNMENT: One characteristic of poetry is repetition of a pattern. In this assignment, the repeated pattern is <u>a series of gerund phrases</u>.

Gerund phrases name things, including ones people like and also dislike. Lots of things—maybe most—have two sides, pleasant/unpleasant, helpful/unhelpful, interesting/boring, healthy/unhealthy, good/bad. Philosophically, that's basic ambivalence, where, for example, sunshine can be sometimes unpleasant but other times pleasant, and rain sometimes pleasant but other times unpleasant.

Think about five things you're ambivalent about, that for you have both plus and minus aspects. For each, write a long gerund phrase to create a five-stanza poem with nothing but gerund phrases.

TOPIC SELECTION: Here are some possibilities, but customize your choices, maybe with some of these, and some of your own.

What I like AND dislike about cars, spiders, beer, love, guys or girls, parents, school, celebrities, pizza, God, Internet, grass, sunshine, rain, puppies, kittens, snakes, kiwi fruit, computers, teeth, hair, fingernails or toenails, clothing (maybe pumps, socks, wedding dresses, tuxedos), malls, weddings, work, IKEA, McDonald's, Baltimore (or another place), TV wrestling, skateboarding, rollerblading, siblings, and so on.

Example: "Yeah and Nay Things"

Yeah magazines: Glimpsing the highlights of news in sports, entertainment, national and world affairs without TV's commercial breaks that jarringly interrupt news, like a groom belching during wedding vows.

Nay magazines: Observing a small ad on a 4 × 6-inch card suddenly falling out of the folds of the magazine where it had been immobile during the shufflings of shipping, but the minute you open the pages slipping out onto your lap.

Process:

- Decide a tone to sustain throughout your gerund poem: serious, humorous, flippant, satiric, philosophical, merry, brooding, sad, joyous, and so on.

- Order the five gerund phrases logically, perhaps from the shortest to the longest, from least to most humorous, from least to most original, or some other arrangement.

- After the fifth stanza (gerund phrase), write a memorable sentence that ties together all of the yes/no comments about your five topics, perhaps making a statement about ambivalence in how people view their own reality.

- Give your gerund poem a clever title.

"There is nothing either good or bad, but thinking makes it so."
—William Shakespeare, *Hamlet*

Infinitive Phrase

In each pair, the second sentence has a noun infinitive. Notice how it adds information and emphasis.

1a. Wet feet meant trouble and danger.
1b. **To get his feet wet in such a freezing temperature** meant trouble and danger. *(Noun infinitive phrase names what was dangerous.)*

> Jack London, "To Build a Fire"

2a. He liked something.
2b. He liked **to pretend that he was carrying a needle full of embalming fluid around with him**. *(Noun infinitive phrase names what he pretended.)*

> Alice Sebold, *The Lovely Bones*

3a. It was their problem.
3b. **To get Janice Avery without ending up squashed or suspended** was their problem. *(Noun infinitive phrase names the problem.)*

> Katherine Paterson, *Bridge to Terabithia*

WHAT IS A NOUN INFINITIVE PHRASE? *It's a phrase that <u>names</u> something and that always begins with* to *plus a verb: to sing, to read, to linger, to laugh, to sigh, to study, and so on.*

Infinitive phrases can name something (like nouns), describe something (like adjectives), or explain a reason for something (like adverbs).

1. *Noun infinitive*—**To make it to the final round of the playoffs** was the team's goal. *The infinitive <u>names</u> the team's goal. Noun infinitives answer the question "What?"*

2. *Adjective infinitive*—The coach emphasized the need **to make it to the final round of the playoffs**. *The infinitive <u>describes</u> the need. Adjective infinitives answer the question "What kind?" (See page 115.)*

3. *Adverb infinitive*—The team from Western High School worked overtime **to make it to the final round of the playoffs**. *The infinitive <u>explains why</u> the team worked overtime. Adverb infinitives answer the question "Why?" (See page 116.)*

Number: Sentences can contain either single or multiple noun infinitives:

*Single—***To be in a place her mother had never seen** was in a way helpful. *(Names what was helpful.)*

> Jhumpa Lahiri, *Unaccustomed Earth*

*Multiple—*Wesley almost told him **to mind his business, to peddle his papers,** and **to put an egg in his shoe and beat it.** *(Names what Wesley almost told him.)*

> Stephen King, *UR*

Position: Because noun infinitive phrases are fixed within a sentence, they cannot be moved to other positions.

PRACTICE 1: MATCHING

Match the noun infinitive with the sentence. Write out each sentence, underlining the noun infinitive.

Sentences:

1. Everything has ^, or else it perishes.

   John Knowles, *A Separate Peace*

2. The stillest hour of the night had come, the hour before dawn, when the world seems ^.

   Kate Chopin, *The Awakening*

3. How freeing it was, these days, ^, with only a single suitcase to check.

   Jhumpa Lahiri, *Unaccustomed Earth*

4. ^ endeared her to a community that thrived on sacrifice.

   Roya Hakakian, *Journey from the Land of No*

5. ^ required enormous effort from the turtle.

   Michael Crichton, *Travels*

Noun Infinitives:

a. to travel alone

b. to say that she had chosen to remain a widow for the sake of her daughters

c. to crawl a hundred yards up the beach, to dig a pit with her clumsy flippers, and to lay her eggs

d. to evolve

e. to hold its breath

PRACTICE 2: UNSCRAMBLING

Rearrange the scrambled list of sentence parts to match the structure of the model. Next, write an imitation of the model. Finally, identify the noun infinitives in the model and your imitation.

MODEL: She told him to take a bath before putting on his new clothes, and not to tell anyone that she had bought them.

Mary Elizabeth Vroman, "See How They Run"

a. that he had allowed this
b. and not to tell the next class
c. he advised them
d. after finishing the first part
e. to skip the second part

PRACTICE 3: COMBINING

Combine the list of sentences into just one sentence that imitates the structure of the model. Next, write an imitation of the model. Finally, identify the noun infinitives in the model and your imitation.

MODEL: She periodically tried to dress the cat in doll clothes and to make it sit at tea parties or picnics.

Gary Paulsen, *The Time Hackers*

a. She sometimes wanted to indulge her daughter.
b. The indulging was in shopping sprees.
c. And she sometimes wanted to let her buy jewelry.
d. The jewelry was from shops and boutiques.

PRACTICE 4: IMITATING

Write an imitation of each model sentence so good that nobody can tell yours from the author's.

Models and Sample Imitations:

1. Children love to play in piles of leaves, hurling them into the air like confetti, leaping into soft unruly mattresses of them.

Diane Ackerman, *A Natural History of the Senses*

Sample: Kids want to dig in mounds of mud, spreading it around the yard like pudding, sliding into slick wet piles of goo.

2. The third man scrabbled away like a crab, slipped into the pool, and then began to climb frantically, to climb up the cliff as the water penciled down.

John Steinbeck, *The Pearl*

Sample: The black spider swung across like an acrobat, landed on the fly, and then started to wrap casually, to wrap up the fly until the gauze enclosed it fully.

3. He taught me to gig for frogs and fish, to find water collected overnight in the hollow of fallen leaves, to distinguish edible mushrooms from deadly toadstools, and dozens of other survival tricks.

Keith Donohue, *The Stolen Child*

Sample: I learned to look for clues and hints, to observe suspects held temporarily in the room for initial questioning, to distinguish plausible lies from outright falsehoods, and lots of essential detective skills.

PRACTICE 5: EXCHANGING

To practice writing good noun infinitives, exchange one of yours for the author's. Try to make yours as good as—maybe even better than—the author's.

Example:

Author's: The children began **to come out of the tents, to wander about the camp.**

John Steinbeck, *The Grapes of Wrath*

Yours: The children began **to run down the beach, to wade in the water.**

1. On the sidewalk Soapy began **to yell drunken gibberish at the top of his harsh voice.**

O. Henry, "The Cop and the Anthem"

2. It became his habit, **to creep out of bed even before his mother was awake, to slip into his clothes,** and **to go quietly down to the barn to see his pony.**

John Steinbeck, *The Red Pony*

3. Grant squeezed his fists together, and bit his lip, trying desperately **to remain motionless, to make no sound to alert the tyrannosaur.**

Michael Crichton, *Jurassic Park*

PRACTICE 6: EXPANDING

Partner with the author by creating an infinitive phrase at the caret (^).

1. All men by nature desire **to ^**.

Aristotle, *Metaphysics*

2. **To ^**, one had to like doing it.

Christy Brown, *My Left Foot*

3. He taught me **to ^, to ^, to ^**.

Perri Knize, *A Piano Odyssey*

COMPOSITION: Resume

ASSIGNMENT: The noun infinitive tool can help in planning and writing a winning resume. Write, revise, or update your resume, perhaps to accompany an application for a job, position, admission, or special program. Include persuasive facts about your skills, abilities, aptitude, personal style, to guarantee your resume survives the screening process.

In the library or on the Internet, learn about planning and writing a good resume. After analyzing effective resumes, list reasons to write a resume. Begin each with a noun infinitive. For example: *To document my writing ability and presentation skill on an important document.*

For part of your resume, use <u>noun infinitive phrases</u> for lists of goals and expected outcomes.

Process:

- List goals for seeking the particular job, position, apprenticeship, scholarship, admission to a graduate program or school, and so on. Begin each goal with a noun infinitive. For example: *To use skills and concepts from my apprenticeship in marine biology to strengthen my candidacy for a position in that field after graduating from college.*

- List experiences you hope to gain if you are selected. For example: *To learn firsthand the process of law by serving as a summer apprentice to a law clerk.*

"Whenever you are asked if you can do a job, tell 'em, 'Certainly I can!'
Then get busy and find out how to do it."
—Theodore Roosevelt, 26th President of the United States

Noun Clause

In each pair, the second sentence has a noun clause. Notice how it adds more information.

1a. He finally decided something.

1b. He finally decided **that children liked dinosaurs because these giant creatures personified the uncontrollable force of looming authority.** *(Noun clause names what he decided.)*

Michael Crichton, Jurassic Park

2a. One of Dad's favorite stories, which he must have told us a hundred times, was about Mom.

2b. One of Dad's favorite stories, which he must have told us a hundred times, was about **how he met and fell in love with Mom.** *(Noun clause names how he met Mom.)*

Jeannette Walls, The Glass Castle

3a. When the old man saw the shark coming, he knew something.

3b. When the old man saw the shark coming, he knew **that this was a shark that had no fear at all and would do exactly what it wished.** *(Noun clause names what he knew.)*

Ernest Hemingway, The Old Man and the Sea

WHAT IS A NOUN CLAUSE? *It's a dependent clause that works like a noun.* Like all clauses, noun clauses contain a subject and its verb.

To understand how noun clauses act like nouns, insert *what we eat for breakfast* into any of these blanks:

1. _____ is important. *(subject)*

2. We discussed _____. *(direct object)*

3. The health teacher talked about _____. *(object of preposition)*

4. A valuable part of a healthy diet is _____. *(predicate noun)*

5. A regular morning meal, _____, provides energy for school. *(appositive)*

Most noun clauses begin with *that, what, how, when, or why*. Some, though, begin with other words. The best way to identify a noun clause is this: if a clause is *not* removable, it is a noun clause.

Removable (adverb or adjective clauses):

1. The exact year **when George Washington was born** was 1732. *(adjective clause)*

2. **When George Washington was born**, cars didn't exist. *(adverb clause)*

Nonremovable (noun clauses):

3. **When George Washington was born** was a question on the quiz.

4. The discussion was about **when George Washington was born.**

5. Mr. Jameson discussed **when George Washington was born.**

Number: Sentences can contain either single or multiple noun clauses:

Single—Her mind only vaguely grasped **what he was saying.**

> Kate Chopin, "A Respectable Woman"

Multiple—As I sat in my corner, I watched **how her hair tumbled about her face when she knelt and chatted with the children, how she brushed it back impatiently with a sweep of her arm.**

> Christy Brown, *My Left Foot*

Position: Because noun clauses are fixed within a sentence, they cannot be moved to other positions.

PRACTICE 1: MATCHING

Match the noun clause with the sentence. Write out each sentence, underlining the noun clause.

Sentences:

1. I wondered ^ because I've always liked them better than the sunrise.
   > Joyce Weatherford, *Heart of the Beast*

2. At the far end of the library, a number of men had gathered into a tight, jostling ring around a very pretty, very young woman who was talking at ^.
   > Michael Chabon, *The Amazing Adventures of Kavalier & Clay*

Noun Clauses:

a. that my father looked nothing like the people around me, and that he was black as pitch, my mother white as milk

b. what we had for food, hardtack and jerky and the few little yellow apples we picked up along the road here and there

3. ^, barely registered in my mind.

    Barack Obama, *Dreams from My Father*

4. He liked ^, surviving even the white heat of cremation.

    Kim Edwards, *The Memory Keeper's Daughter*

5. I was carrying ^, and our changes of shirts and socks, all by then filthy.

    Marilynne Robinson, *Gilead*

c. why she hated sunsets so much

d. that bones were solid things

e. what must have been the top of her lungs

PRACTICE 2: UNSCRAMBLING

Rearrange the scrambled list of sentence parts to match the structure of the model. Next, write an imitation of the model. Finally, identify the noun clauses in the model and your imitation.

MODEL: While he was sitting with her on the side of the bed, Mary came to the door and said that the missus wanted to see him in the parlor.

James Joyce, "The Boarding House"

    a. the quarterback sat on the bench
    b. when he was listening to the coach
    c. after the end of the game
    d. that his team chose to ignore him on the field
    e. and saw

PRACTICE 3: COMBINING

Combine the list of sentences into just one sentence that imitates the structure of the model. Next, write an imitation of the model. Finally, identify the noun clauses in the model and your imitation.

MODEL: Florence suspected that there was something profoundly wrong with her, that she had always been different, and that at last she was about to be exposed.

Ian McEwan, *On Chesil Beach*

    a. Juan realized three things about Jorge.
    b. One was that there was something very different about Jorge.
    c. Another was that Jorge had always been chosen.
    d. And another was that now he was going to be rejected.

PRACTICE 4: IMITATING

Write an imitation of each model sentence so good that nobody can tell yours from the author's.

Models and Sample Imitations:

1. I said that English was my best subject.

> J. D. Salinger, *The Catcher in the Rye*

Sample: I understood why sleep was so very important.

2. Phyllis wrote about how her family gathered the night Neil Armstrong landed on the moon, and how they shuttled between the living room television and the bedroom where her father was dying.

> Frank McCourt, *Teacher Man*

Sample: Harry talked about how his class celebrated the day after they graduated from high school, and how they fluctuated between the long-awaited joy and the letdown after the ceremony was over.

3. Kirsti had gone to bed reluctantly, complaining that she wanted to stay up with the others, that she was grown-up enough, that she had never before seen a dead person in a closed-up box, that it wasn't fair.

> Lois Lowry, *Number the Stars*

Sample: Steve had begun to tap automatically, demonstrating that he knew how to keep up with the band, that he was skillful enough, that he had slowly learned the Gene Krupa technique from some old recordings, that it was exciting.

PRACTICE 5: EXCHANGING

To practice writing good noun clauses, exchange one of yours for the author's. Try to make yours as good as—maybe even better than—the author's.

Example:

Author's: Like all instructors of English, he thought **that he had a novel in him somewhere and would write it someday**.

> Stephen King, *UR*

Yours: Like all instructors of English, he thought **that he would inspire his students and would teach them love of language.**

---

1. **What had come out** was also amazing.

   Stephen King, *Bag of Bones*

2. It pained him **that he did not know well what politics meant** and **that he did not know where the universe ended.**

   James Joyce, *Portrait of the Artist as a Young Man*

3. He understood **who was running numbers, who was running games, and who was square and respectable.**

   Maya Angelou, *The Heart of a Woman*

PRACTICE 6: EXPANDING

Partner with the author by creating a noun clause at the caret (^).

1. **How** ^ is a mystery not easily to be solved.

   John Steinbeck, *The Pearl*

2. When the children went on a hike, she packed bird and flower guides into their knapsacks, and quizzed them on their return to see **if** ^.

   Wallace Stegner, *Crossing to Safety*

3. Mortenson told the crowd now watching him with rapt attention **that** ^, **that** ^, **that** ^.

   Greg Mortenson and David Oliver Relin, *Three Cups of Tea*

COMPOSITION: Political Speech

ASSIGNMENT: Your instructor may have commented on one of your papers something like this: "Not parallel" or "Use parallel structure." Such comments refer to a desirable style called *parallel structure,* using the same kind of tool for each item in a series.

Pretend you are a politician seeking office or an elected official writing a speech to be broadcast on television to millions of people. As part of that speech, use sentences containing parallel structure, perhaps in imitation of the examples given below.

Include in your paper at least three sentences with <u>a series of noun clauses expressed in parallel structure</u>.

The first sentence of the "Declaration of Independence" is a famous example of parallel structure with multiple noun clauses. All of those clauses begin with the word *that* to name the self-evident truths.

We hold these truths to be self-evident:
***that** all men are created equal,*
***that** they are endowed by their Creator with certain unalienable rights,*
***that** among these are life, liberty and the pursuit of happiness,*
***that** to secure these rights, governments are instituted among men, deriving their just powers from the consent of the governed,*
***that** whenever any form of government becomes destructive of these ends, it is the right of the people to alter or to abolish it, and to institute new government, laying its foundation on such principles and organizing its powers in such form, as to them shall seem most likely to effect their safety and happiness.*

Here is a sentence by President Barack Obama illustrating multiple noun clauses expressed in parallel structure.

I know the desperation and disorder of the powerless:
***how** it twists the lives of children on the streets of Jakarta or Nairobi in much the same way as it does the lives of children on Chicago's South Side,*
***how** narrow the path is for them between humiliation and untrammeled fury,*
***how** easily they slip into violence and despair.*

Barack Obama, *Dreams from My Father*

Process:

- Introduce your speech by stating the importance of what it will contain.

- Include a sentence with a parallel series of noun clauses, each beginning with one of these words: *that, how, who, why*

- Continue with these three paragraphs:

  - description of a problem facing the people;

  - proposal of a solution to that problem; and

  - invocation of the help of the audience in reaching that solution.

- Conclude with a paragraph that provides a hope for the future, with an emphatic optimism that, with everyone working together, all will be well.

"Eloquence is the essential thing in a speech, not information."
—Mark Twain, author

Reviewing the Noun Tools

This section reviews all of the sentence-composing tools from the noun group. You'll study the sentences of famous writer Stephen King. Author of over seventy books, and recipient in 2003 of the National Book Foundation Medal for Distinguished Contribution to American Letters, King received high praise from the judges:

> *Stephen King's writing is securely rooted in the great American tradition that glorifies spirit-of-place and the abiding power of narrative. He crafts stylish, mindbending page-turners that contain profound moral truths—some beautiful, some harrowing—about our inner lives. This Award commemorates Mr. King's wellearned place of distinction in the wide world of readers and book lovers of all ages.*

In this review, analyzing sentences from Stephen King's works, you'll identify the noun tools, and then imitate several of his sentences. Study how Stephen King skillfully builds his sentences, using the noun tools you've learned.

"Try to remember that grammar is for the world as well as for school."
Stephen King, *Everything's Eventual*

Directions: Using these abbreviations, identify the underlined tools. If you need to review the tool, study the pages below.

NOUN TOOLS	Review These Pages
appositive phrase= AP	Pages 29–33
gerund phrase = G	Pages 35–41
infinitive phrase = INF *(noun)*	Pages 43–47
noun clause = NC	Pages 49–55

REVIEW 1: IDENTIFYING NOUN TOOLS————————————

1. The clock by the stove, <u>one of Jo's rare lapses into bad taste</u>, is Felix the Cat.
   —*Bag of Bones*

2. None of them knew <u>that Carrie White was telekinetic</u>.
   —*Carrie*

3. His Mom had taught him the dozen basic things he knew about cooking, and one of them had to do with the art of <u>making grilled cheese sandwiches</u>.

   —*Dreamcatcher*

4. Wesley almost told him <u>to mind his business, to peddle his papers, to put an egg in his shoe and beat it</u>.

   —*UR*

5. My own father was still alive, <u>a hale and genially profane man of seventy-four</u>.

   —*From a Buick 8: A Novel*

6. He believed the only three valid purposes microwaves served were <u>re-heating coffee, making popcorn</u>, and <u>putting a buzz under take-out from places like Cluck-Cluck Tonite</u>.

   —*Needful Things*

7. Dad wanted me <u>to lug wood for the cook-stove, to weed the beans and cukes, to pitch hay out of the loft, to get two jugs of water to put in the pantry</u>, and <u>to scrape as much old paint off the cellar bulkhead as I could</u>.

   —*Everything's Eventual*

8. The sound it made was a silky whisper, and <u>watching it</u> was like <u>watching an evil magic carpet</u>.

   —*Bag of Bones*

9. I knew <u>that you wanted a bicycle, that getting one was very important to you</u>, and <u>that you meant to earn the money for one this summer</u>.

   —*Hearts in Atlantis*

10. In the cellar, smells of dirt and wet and long-gone vegetables would merge into one unmistakable smell, <u>the smell of monster, the apotheosis of all monsters, the smell of something for which he had no name, the smell of IT</u>, crouched and lurking and ready to spring, <u>a creature which would eat anything but which was especially hungry for boymeat</u>.

    —*It*

REVIEW 2: IMITATING

For each model sentence, write the letter of its imitation. Then write your own imitation of the same model.

Group 1: Model Sentences

1. The clock by the stove, one of Jo's rare lapses into bad taste, is Felix the Cat.

2. None of them knew that Carrie White was telekinetic.

3. His Mom had taught him the dozen basic things he knew about cooking, and one of them had to do with the art of making grilled cheese sandwiches.

4. Wesley almost told him to mind his business, to peddle his papers, to put an egg in his shoe and beat it.

5. My own father was still alive, a hale and genially profane man of seventy-four.

Group 1: Imitations

a. All of the class thought that Stewpot Stuart was quirky.

b. A friend had shown her the few simple tricks she knew about makeup, and some of the techniques were about the illusion of lengthening barely visible brown eyelashes.

c. His only brother had remained around, a kind and reliably helpful man with unlimited generosity.

d. The picture in Barbara's wallet, testimony to an infrequent venture into sentimentality, is Annie the puppy.

e. The housekeeper manager patiently reminded her to launder the sheets, to fold the towels, to clean the mirror in the bathroom and shine it.

Group 2: Model Sentences

6. He believed the only three valid purposes microwaves served were re-heating coffee, making popcorn, and putting a buzz under take-out from places like Cluck-Cluck Tonite.

7. Dad wanted me to lug wood for the cook-stove, to weed the beans and cukes, to pitch hay out of the loft, to get two jugs of water to put in the pantry, and to scrape as much old paint off the cellar bulkhead as I could.

8. The sound it made was a silky whisper, and watching it was like watching an evil magic carpet.

9. I knew that you wanted a bicycle, that getting one was very important to you, and that you meant to earn the money for one this summer.

10. In the cellar, smells of dirt and wet and long-gone vegetables would merge into one unmistakable smell, the smell of monster, the apotheosis of all monsters, the smell of something for which he had no name, the smell of IT, crouched and lurking and ready to spring, a creature which would eat anything but which was especially hungry for boymeat.

Group 2: Imitations

f. She learned that he selected a house, that choosing one was the beginning for them, and that he promised to make the place all theirs this week.

g. In the summer, sounds of laughter and chatter and friendly familiar voices would contribute to one memorable impression, the impression of leisure, the conglomeration of nonstop fun, the culmination of everything for which he had waited, the relaxation of vacation unhurried and joyous and easy to live, a vacation which would please everyone but which was especially thrilling for the kids.

h. She understood the truly fundamental, unshakable reasons friendship mattered were sharing memories, keeping secrets, and enjoying some laughter over silly mistakes in clothing like fashion fiascos.

i. The boss told her to get water for the stable horses, to feed the dogs and cats, to distribute grain in the stalls, to fill several wheelbarrows with manure to use in the garden, and to brush down as many of the horses in the barn as she could.

j. The smell it released was a Jasmine scent, and sniffing it was like sniffing an enticing, tropical flower.

Previewing the Verb Tools

Verbs usually <u>narrate</u>. This section introduces you to the verb group of sentence-composing tools: phrases that tell what someone or something did.

After this introduction, you'll focus on two particular narrating tools in the verb group, learn about each tool in depth, practice using the tool through varied activities, and apply the tool in a piece of your writing.

SINGLE VERB	MULTIPLE VERB	INVERTED VERB
The aroma of pizza <u>**filled**</u> the restaurant.	The aroma of pizza <u>**filled**</u> the restaurant and <u>**tempted**</u> the dieter.	**From the brick oven** <u>came</u> the aroma of pizza.

Verb Tools—There are two kinds of verb tools used sometimes by skillful writers: multiple verb and inverted verb. Like most verbs, those two tools narrate what someone or something did.

---

1. **Multiple Verb**—Narrates a series of actions

Examples:

I <u>put on my pajamas, read for a while</u>, and <u>found myself suddenly unable to keep my eyes open</u>. *(Narrates three actions.)*
Harper Lee, To Kill a Mockingbird

Then I <u>flung myself onto my bed, tore off my left shoe, ripped off my left sock with the other foot, seized a pencil between my first and second left toes</u>, and <u>began to write</u>. *(Narrates five actions.)*
Christy Brown, My Left Foot

Pakhow <u>drew out his money, placed it on the cap, unfastened his belt, took off his outer coat, girded his belt tightly over his stomach again, put a bag of bread inside his jacket, tied a flask of water to his belt, drew his bootlegs tight, took the spade from his laborer</u>, and <u>got set to go</u>. *(Narrates ten actions.)*
Leo Tolstoy, "How Much Land Does a Man Need?"

---

2. **Inverted Verb**—Reverses the usual order (the subject before the verb) by putting the verb before the subject. (Subjects are <u>underlined</u>, and verbs are in **boldface**.)

Examples:

There, lying to one side of an immense bed, **lay** <u>grandpa</u>.

> Katherine Mansfield, "The Voyage"

In the shark's stomach **were** <u>bottles, knives, tin cans, chunks of wood</u>, and <u>pieces of iron</u>.

> Willard Price, "The Killer Shark"

On a tarnished gilt easel before the fireplace **stood** <u>a crayon portrait of Miss Emily's father</u>.

> William Faulkner, "A Rose for Emily"

With the Valar **came** <u>other spirits of the same order as the Valar but of less degree</u>.

> J. R. R. Tolkien, *Silmarillion*

Review

Directions: For sentences with **boldfaced** *verb tools*, exchange one of your own for the author's. For sentences with *deleted* *verb tools*, expand the sentence by adding one of your own at the caret (^).

EXAMPLE OF EXCHANGING

Author's: Bobby **ran into the bathroom, got a facecloth from the shelf by the tub,** and **wet it in cold water.**

> Stephen King, *Hearts in Atlantis*

Yours: Bobby **jumped over the hedges, did a cartwheel on the lawn near the tool shed,** and **surprised his girlfriend with his presence.**

EXAMPLE OF EXPANDING

Author's Sentence with Deleted Tool: Through the long white corridors that led to the staterooms of the Titanic **came** ^.

Your Added Tool: Through the long white corridors that led to the staterooms of the Titanic **came a sudden river that rose up the walls of the hall like a giant bathtub.**

Original Sentence: Through the long white corridors that led to the staterooms of the Titanic **came only the murmurs of people trapped.**

Walter Lord, A Night to Remember

Multiple Verb: Exchange the first five. Expand the next five.

1. The walls **bent, rocked, cracked.**

   Fritz Leiber, "A Bad Day for Sales"

2. The king **gripped the arms of his chair, closed his eyes, clenched his teeth, and sweated.**

   T. S. White, The Book of Merlyn

3. Suddenly, she **snatched herself from the young man's soft and timid embrace, seemed to listen to something, and, with a quick gesture, pointed to the door.**

   Gaston Leroux, The Phantom of the Opera

4. Sighing, I **scooped up the small creature, placed him on the bottom step, and went back to my cot.**

   Harper Lee, To Kill a Mockingbird

5. Mrs. Jones **stopped, jerked him around in front of her, put a half nelson about his neck,** and **continued to drag him up the street.**

   Langston Hughes, "Thank You, M'am"

6. His dog ^ and ^, yelping with pleasure.

   Allegra Goodman, Intuition

7. One day, in tears, I ^, ^, and ^.

   Christy Brown, My Left Foot

8. Every hour he ^, ^, ^, and ^.

   Elliott Merrick, "Without Words"

9. The men on the porch ^, ^, ^, ^, ^.

   Ray Bradbury, *The Martian Chronicles*

10. He ^, ^, ^, ^, ^, and then ^.

    Franz Kafka, "In the Penal Colony"

Inverted Verb: Exchange the first five. Expand the next five.

11. Crossing that ground was **a large tailless dog, black in color.**

    Cormac McCarthy, *No Country for Old Men*

12. From all the other houses down the street **came sounds of music, pianos playing, doors slamming.**

    Ray Bradbury, *The Martian Chronicles*

13. In front of him **loomed the backdrop of high snow-covered mountains, perfect in their majesty, dressed in heavily wooded forests.**

    William P. Young, *The Shack*

14. Standing in the truck bed, holding onto the bars of the sides, **rode the others, twelve-year-old Ruthie and ten-year-old Winfield, grime-faced and wild, their eyes tired but excited.**

    John Steinbeck, *The Grapes of Wrath*

15. Somewhere there, on that desolate plain, **was lurking this fiendish man, hiding in a burrow like a wild beast, his heart full of malignancy against the whole race which had cast him out.**

    Sir Arthur Conan Doyle, *The Hound of the Baskervilles*

16. On the back of his sweatshirt, drawn in bright red ink, **was** ^.

    Stephen King, *Hearts in Atlantis*

17. From every window **came** ^.

    Ray Bradbury, *Dandelion Wine*

18. One of the girls in yellow was playing the piano, and beside her **stood** ^.

    F. Scott Fitzgerald, *The Great Gatsby*

19. Appearing frightened and defiant **were** ^.

    Glendon Swarthout, *Bless the Beasts and Children*

20. A tall boy with glittering golden hair and a sulky mouth pushed and jostled a light wheel chair along, in which **sat** ^.

    Katherine Anne Porter, *Ship of Fools*

"After the verb to love, to help *is the most beautiful verb in the world."*
—Bertha von Suttner, first woman to win the Nobel Peace Prize

---

In the next pages, you'll learn and practice how authors use each of the tools in the verb group to build their sentences, and how you can use them, too.

Multiple Verb

In each pair, the second sentence has a multiple verb. Notice how additional verbs give readers much more information about what is happening.

1a. He spat dryly.
1b. He spat dryly **and wiped his mouth on the shoulder of his cotton workshirt.** *(two verbs)*

> Cormac McCarthy, *No Country for Old Men*

2a. They filled their plates.
2b. They filled their plates, **poured bacon gravy over the biscuits, and sugared their coffee.** *(three verbs)*

> John Steinbeck, *The Grapes of Wrath*

3a. The man opposite me took off his spectacles.
3b. The man opposite me took off his spectacles, **put them away in a case, folded his paper,** and **put it in his pocket.** *(four verbs)*

> Ernest Hemingway, *A Farewell to Arms*

WHAT IS A MULTIPLE VERB? *It's one in a series of verbs telling what the subject is doing.* Multiple verbs always answer this question: What series of actions did the subject do?

Punctuation: Two verb phrases are usually joined by *and*. For more than two, put a comma after each verb phrase:

Two verb phrases—At nine o'clock, one morning late in July, Gatsby's gorgeous car **lurched up the rocky drive to my door** and **gave out a burst of melody from its three-noted horn.**

> F. Scott Fitzgerald, *The Great Gatsby*

More than two verb phrases—After their father's death, the girls **hovered around her, watched everything she did, followed her through the house,** and **got in her way.** *(The comma before* and *is optional, but most writers include it.)*

> Marilynne Robinson, *Housekeeping*

PRACTICE 1: MATCHING

Match the multiple verb with the sentence. Write out each sentence.

Sentences:

1. While Dudley lolled around watching and eating ice cream, Harry cleaned the windows, ^.

   J. K. Rowling, *Harry Potter and the Chamber of Secrets*

2. When the headaches struck, the general went to his room, ^.

   Khaled Hosseini, *The Kite Runner*

3. The corpse detail carried the bodies to a clearing outside, ^.

   John Hersey, *Hiroshima*

4. She set the little creature down ^.

   Lewis Carroll, *Alice's Adventures in Wonderland*

5. Then she reached down toward him, ^.

   Langston Hughes, "Thank You, M'am"

Multiple Verbs:

a. and felt quite relieved to see it trot away quietly into the woods

b. picked the boy up by his shirt front, and shook him until his teeth rattled

c. washed the car, mowed the lawn, trimmed the flowerbeds, pruned and watered the roses, and repainted the garden bench

d. undressed, turned off the light, locked the door, and didn't come out until the pain subsided

e. placed them on pyres of wood from ruined houses, burned them, put some of the ashes in envelopes intended for exposed X-ray plates, marked the envelopes with the names of the deceased, and piled them, neatly and respectfully, in stacks in the office

PRACTICE 2: UNSCRAMBLING

Rearrange the scrambled list of sentence parts to match the structure of the model. Next, write an imitation of the model. Finally, identify the multiple verbs in the model and your imitation.

MODEL: To remove the pus, he picked up a sharp blade of stone and scraped at the wound, sawed at the proud flesh, and then squeezed the green juice out in big drops.

John Steinbeck, "Flight"

    a. and then unwrapped the paper-thin cellophane around the large roast
    b. looked at the wrapped package
    c. she took out the frozen piece of meat
    d. to begin the preparation
    e. and cleaned off the counter

PRACTICE 3: COMBINING

Combine the list of sentences into just one sentence that imitates the structure of the model. Next, write an imitation of the model. Finally, identify the multiple verbs in the model and your imitation.

MODEL: Finally, she made her decision, drew a long, rattling breath, picked up the phone again, and dialed.

Ronald Rogers, "The Good Run"

    a. Tentatively, Ambrose gave his answer.
    b. As he gave it, he analyzed the dense, thorny problem.
    c. Also, he waited for the response patiently.
    d. And he hoped.

PRACTICE 4: IMITATING

Write an imitation of each model sentence so good that nobody can tell yours from the author's.

Models and Sample Imitations:

1. A boulder the size of a three-story house accelerated, bouncing and spinning down a slope of loose stones, then pulverized an iceberg on the trail ahead of him.

Greg Mortenson and David Oliver Relin, *Three Cups of Tea*

Sample: An explosion the size of a log fire ignited, torching and eating up a small path of dry twigs, then traveled that path through the woods to the car.

2. He paused, examined my expression, and, seeing that he had won me over, lowered himself into a chair, to rest at last.

Roya Hakakian, Journey from the Land of No

Sample: He stopped, closed his mouth, and, finding that he could not swallow, excused himself from the table, to regurgitate in private.

3. He blessed himself and climbed quickly into bed and, tucking the end of the nightshirt under his feet, curled himself together under the cold white sheets, shaking and trembling.

James Joyce, Portrait of the Artist as a Young Man

Sample: She dressed herself and walked quietly toward breakfast, and, sniffing the aroma of the pancakes from the kitchen, hastened her steps toward the warm, aromatic kitchen, imagining and anticipating.

PRACTICE 5: EXCHANGING

To practice writing good multiple verbs, exchange one of yours for the author's. Try to make yours as good as—maybe even better than—the author's.

Example:

Author's: They stopped daydreaming **and swiftly got down to business, giving orders**.

Toni Morrison, Song of Solomon

Yours: They stopped daydreaming **and immediately made decisions, making progress**.

1. They carried their shoes down the hall **and stopped at the top landing**.

Kent Haruf, Plainsong

2. In the darkness in the hallway by the door, the sick woman arose **and started again toward her own room**.

Sherwood Anderson, Winesburg, Ohio

3. Dad peeled through the town at a hundred miles an hour, **ran a red light, cut the wrong way up a one-way street, with the other cars honking and pulling over.**

> Jeannette Walls, *The Glass Castle*

PRACTICE 6: EXPANDING

Partner with the author to create a verb at each caret (^).

1. The fallen rider twitched once and ^.

> Khaled Hosseini, *The Kite Runner*

2. By age four, I was pretty good with Dad's pistol, a big black six-shot revolver, and could ^.

> Jeannette Walls, *The Glass Castle*

3. Grandma laid linoleum, ^, ^, ^, and ^.

> Ray Bradbury, "Good-bye, Grandma"

COMPOSITION: Cinematic Paragraph

ASSIGNMENT: Multiple verbs convey a cinematic view of action, allowing readers to imagine clearly the scene. Write a narrative paragraph from a picture or an electronic image showing a person performing lots of action: consider something from sports, history, entertainment, or current events. Include in your paragraph <u>at least two sentences containing multiple verbs</u>, with one sentence having more than three verbs.

Process:

- Start the paragraph with a sentence identifying the scene.

- Continue by zooming in on the multiple actions of the person featured in the scene.

- Conclude by zooming out for a dramatic ending that will linger in your reader's memory.

"Life is a verb."
—Charlotte Perkins

"Love is a verb."
—Clare Booth Luce

"God is a verb."
—Richard Buckminster Fuller

Inverted Verb

In each pair, the second sentence has an inverted verb. Notice how the unusual arrangement—verb placed before its subject—draws added attention, zooming in on the subject near the end of the sentence.

Note: Subjects are <u>underlined</u>; verbs are **boldface**.

1a. Over their heads <u>great chandeliers</u> **swung**.

1b. Over their heads **swung** <u>great chandeliers</u>.

        Christy Brown, *My Left Foot*

2a. On another tray, <u>thick sandwiches of rich chicken meat and fresh cut tomatoes and green onions</u> **stood**.

2b. On another tray **stood** <u>thick sandwiches of rich chicken meat and fresh cut tomatoes and green onions</u>.

        Ray Bradbury, *The Illustrated Man*

3a. <u>A girl</u> **was** lying face downwards quite still on the ground, with her arms clasping the trunk of a large tree.

3b. Lying face downwards quite still on the ground, with her arms clasping the trunk of a large tree, **was** <u>a girl</u>.

        Elizabeth Howard, "Three Miles Up"

WHAT IS AN INVERTED VERB? *It's a verb placed after the subject rather than before it.* Inverted verbs peak the reader's curiosity by placing emphasis on the subject located near the end of the sentence.

Verb Group: The Narrating Tools

PRACTICE 1: MATCHING

Match the subject with the sentence. Write out each sentence.

Sentences:

1. Down the steps and upon the platform pounded ^.

   Henry Sydnor Harrison, "Miss Hinch"

2. From the far side of the hill, where Wilma was being buried, came ^.

   Stephen King, *Needful Things*

3. Bounding down from branch to branch till he was just above their heads came ^.

   C. S. Lewis, *The Chronicles of Narnia*

4. Tethered to the rear of the wagon stood ^.

   Conrad Richter, "Early Marriage"

5. The thing for Daisy to do was to rush out of the house, child in arms, but apparently there were ^.

   F. Scott Fitzgerald, *The Great Gatsby*

Subjects:

a. no such intentions in her head

b. the most magnificent red squirrel that Caspian had ever seen

c. the feet of three flying policemen

d. the sound of many voices rising and falling in response to Father John Brigham

e. her saddle mare, Fancy, with pricked-up ears

PRACTICE 2: UNSCRAMBLING

Rearrange the scrambled list of sentence parts to match the structure of the model. Next, write an imitation of the model. Finally, identify the inverted verbs in the model and your imitation.

MODEL: On the other end of the dining room was a tall marble fireplace, always lit by the orange glow of a fire in the wintertime.

   Khaled Hosseini, *The Kite Runner*

   a. of a child in the house
   b. in the dark corner of the old mansion
   c. was a forgotten Teddy bear
   d. never cuddled by the small hand

PRACTICE 3: COMBINING

Combine the list of sentences into just one sentence that imitates the structure of the model. Next, write an imitation of the model. Finally, identify the inverted verbs in the model and your imitation.

MODEL: Beside the desk, in a dark blue dress sat Ariadne, looking somber and beautiful.

Harry Petrakis, "The Wooing of Ariadne"

a. It happened against the window.
b. It happened in a slate gray sky.
c. In that sky came rain.
d. The rain was tapping gently and rhythmically.

PRACTICE 4: IMITATING

Write an imitation of each model sentence so good that nobody can tell yours from the author's.

Models and Sample Imitations:

1. Ahead, glittering like a mirror, was the hotdog wagon.

Stephen King, *Hearts in Atlantis*

Sample: Overhead, heating like an oven, was the unforgiving sun.

2. Along the empty avenues of this town, now whistling softly, kicking a tin can ahead of him in deepest concentration, came a tall, thin man.

Ray Bradbury, *The Martian Chronicles*

Sample: Beside the worn path toward the lake, now slithering quietly, turning its oblong head toward the sound of approaching footsteps, slid a poisonous, hidden snake.

3. In the falling quiet was no sky or earth, only snow lifting in the wind, frosting the window glass, chilling the rooms, deadening and hushing the city.

Truman Capote, "Miriam"

Sample: In the setting sun was no light or luster, just color reflecting on the water, contrasting the dark ocean, calming the horizon, outlining and painting the clouds.

PRACTICE 5: EXCHANGING

To practice writing good inverted verbs, exchange one of yours plus its subject for the author's. Try to make yours as good as—maybe even better than—the author's.

Example:

Author's: Riding the rope that pulled the bell **was Doris Anne, giggling with unbridled delight.**

> Mildred D. Taylor, *Let the Circle Be Unbroken*

Yours: Riding the rope that pulled the bell **was the hunchback of Notre Dame church, swinging with frenzied speed.**

1. Below the pulpit **stood the casket, pearly gray, decorated with a spray of white flowers.**

   > Anne Tyler, *Saint Maybe*

2. In Mama's house **was a large parlor built by my grandfather to his wife's exact specifications so that it was always cool, facing away from the sun.**

   > Judith Ortiz Cofer, *Silent Dancing*

3. In the park at the end of the block **is an enormous canvas tent, thickly striped in white and magenta with an unmistakable peaked top.**

   > Sara Gruen, *Water for Elephants*

PRACTICE 6: EXPANDING

Partner with the author to create a subject at the caret (^).

1. In the kitchen of the apartment in Green Point were ^.

   > J. M. Coetzee, *Disgrace*

2. Over the table, where a collection of cloth samples was scattered, hung ^.

   > Franz Kafka, *The Metamorphosis*

3. On the porch were ^.

   > Flannery O'Connor, "The River"

COMPOSITION: Photographic Paragraph

ASSIGNMENT: Inverted verbs often draw a picture of a place, as in the model paragraph by John Steinbeck. He gives readers a verbal photograph of a bunkhouse dormitory where hired ranch hands live. He uses <u>inverted verbs in six of the seven sentences</u> to emphasize the details of the bunkhouse.

Write a seven-sentence paragraph describing a place—perhaps your room, a restaurant, a study hall, a classroom, a place of worship, and so on. The sentences in your paragraph should imitate the sentences from the model

Model Photographic Paragraph

(1) Inside a long, rectangular building, the bunkhouse had whitewashed walls and an unpainted floor. (2) In three walls there were small, square windows, and in the fourth, a solid door with a wooden latch. (3) Against the walls were eight bunk beds, five of them made up with blankets, the other three unmade, exposing the burlap ticking on their mattresses. (4) Over each bunk there was nailed a wooden apple crate, containing two wooden shelves for the personal possessions of the occupant of the bunk. (5) On these shelves were loaded little articles: soap, shaving cream, combs, brushes, razors, and medicines. (6) Near one wall there was a wood stove, its stovepipe going straight up through the ceiling. (7) In the middle of the room stood a big square table, littered with playing cards, and around it were wooden apple boxes for the card players to sit on.

John Steinbeck, *Of Mice and Men*

Process:

- Begin with a sentence that identifies the place to be described.

- Decide on and follow an organization: up to down, left to right, least important to most important, or other arrangement.

- Continue by zooming in on items within that place, describing in detail one object at a time.

"I see pictures in the poorest of huts and the dirtiest of corners."
—Vincent van Gogh, artist

Reviewing the Verb Tools

This section reviews all of the sentence-composing tools from the verb group through sentences of famous author Stephen King. Miraculous survivor of a near-fatal accident in which a truck hit him at night as he walked along a road, King struggled through a long recuperation. Media reports concluded that his writing days were over, but King rebounded, and wrote a nonfiction work titled *On Writing*, an accessible, clear guide to better writing. He also subsequently wrote novels, screenplays, columns for magazines, and a fascinating website on his life and works, making Stephen King one of the world's most prolific, popular, and successful writers.

In this review, analyzing sentences from Stephen King's works, you'll identify the verb tools and then imitate several of his sentences. Study how Stephen King skillfully builds his sentences, using the verb tools you've learned.

Directions: Using these abbreviations, identify the underlined tools. If you need to review the tool, study the pages below.

VERB TOOLS	Review These Pages
multiple verb = MV	Pages 67–71
inverted verb = IV	Pages 73–77

REVIEW 1: IDENTIFYING VERB TOOLS

1. A long-fingered hand, as white as the hand of a corpse, <u>reached up in the gloom,</u> <u>found the ring-pull which hung down</u>, and <u>drew the shade</u>.
   —*Needful Things*

2. From his left hand <u>swung the handles of an artist's portfolio</u>, the kind that closes and latches to make a traveling case.
   —*Cell: A Novel*

3. I <u>sat up against the pillows, rubbed my eyes, and saw a dark, shouldery shape</u>, standing between me and the window.
   —*Bag of Bones*

4. Clutched in his big, knuckly hands <u>was a matted piece of fur</u>.
   —*Needful Things*

5. In the recess <u>was a silk hair-ribbon his lady had given him, a packet of letters she had written him, a few letters from him to her which burned so brightly he did not dare to send them</u>, and <u>a little locket with his mother's picture inside it</u>.

    —*The Eyes of the Dragon*

6. The boy <u>plunged his hands up to the wrists in the mud of Wilma Jerzyck's garden</u> and <u>then flung that mud at Wilma Jerzyck's clean sheets on the clothes line in her yard again and again and again</u>.

    —*Needful Things*

7. From the far side of the hill, where Wilma Jerzyck was being buried at the same time, <u>came the sound of many voices rising and falling in response to Father John Brigham</u>.

    —*Needful Things*

8. Halfway to the top I <u>slipped to my knees, looked over my shoulder</u>, and <u>saw the man in the black suit almost at my heels</u>, his white face pulling into a convulsion of fury and greed.

    —*Everything's Eventual*

9. Ceremoniously crossed above this fabulous trophy <u>were Roland's great bow and the arrow Foe-Hammer</u>, its tip and shaft still black with dragon blood.

    —*The Eyes of the Dragon*

10. He <u>raises money for environmental causes, speaks on college campuses from that snazzy red wheelchair, defends the eco-activists in court when they need defending</u>.

    —*Hearts in Atlantis*

REVIEW 2: IMITATING

For each model sentence, write the letter of its imitation. Then write your own imitation of the same model.

Group 1: Model Sentences

1. A long-fingered hand, as white as the hand of a corpse, reached up in the gloom, found the ring-pull which hung down, and drew the shade.

2. From his left hand swung the handles of an artist's portfolio, the kind that closes and latches to make a traveling case.

3. I sat up against the pillows, rubbed my eyes, and saw a dark, shouldery shape, standing between me and the window.

4. Clutched in his big, knuckly hands was a matted piece of fur.

5. In the recess was a silk hair-ribbon his lady had given him, a packet of letters she had written him, a few letters from him to her which burned so brightly he did not dare to send them, and a little locket with his mother's picture inside it.

Group 1: Imitations

a. I arose from my chair, searched the hotel lobby, and found my missing leather wallet, sticking out between the sofa's cushion and its back.

b. Hidden in the shadowed top shelf was a lost memento of my grandfather.

c. A heavily-speckled scarf, as ugly as the back of a snake, drifted down the steps, touched the railing which bordered them, and lifted her gaze.

d. On the table was a gourmet dinner his wife had made him, a bouquet of flowers she had brought him, a few messages from her to him which read so lovingly he could only hope to treasure them, and a chocolate cake with buttercream icing on top.

e. From Akeela's small arms hung the limbs of a stuffed monkey, the toy that comforts and snuggles to make a perfect companion.

Group 2: Model Sentences

6. The boy plunged his hands up to the wrists in the mud of Wilma Jerzyck's garden and then flung that mud at Wilma Jerzyck's clean sheets on the clothes line in her yard again and again and again.

7. From the far side of the hill, where Wilma Jerzyck was being buried at the same time, came the sound of many voices, rising and falling in response to Father John Brigham.

8. Halfway to the top I slipped to my knees, looked over my shoulder, and saw the man in the black suit almost at my heels, his white face pulling into a convulsion of fury and greed.

9. Ceremoniously crossed above this fabulous trophy were Roland's great bow and the arrow Foe-Hammer, its tip and shaft still black with dragon blood.

10. He raises money for environmental causes, speaks on college campuses from that snazzy red wheelchair, defends the eco-activists in court when they need defending.

Group 2: Imitations

f. Over the unblemished field by the church, where they were being married in the clear sunlight, rose the scores of released butterflies, lifting and wafting in celebration of their vows.

g. Gently placed near her wedding dress were the antique lace veil and the satin slippers, their heels and toes still pristine after the walk down the aisle.

h. Close to the finish I pumped up my speed, glanced behind me, and heard the runner in the position nearest to me, her ragged breath forcing out an effort of intensity and pride.

i. The woman masterminded the robbery with masks on the faces of each culprit and then buried those masks in her own backyard under the maple tree beside the porch immediately and secretly and deeply.

j. Connie watches children for working mothers, plays on backyard jungle gyms with constant unfailing good humor, holds any disgruntled children in her arms when they need holding.

Previewing the Adjective Tools

Adjectives <u>describe</u>. This section introduces you to the adjective group of sentence-composing tools: words, phrases, and clauses that *describe* someone or something.

After this introduction, you'll focus on the particular describing tools in the adjective group, learn about each tool in depth, practice using the tool through varied activities, and apply the tool in a piece of your writing.

ADJECTIVE WORDS	ADJECTIVE PHRASES	ADJECTIVE CLAUSES
The dog, **asleep**, was on the forbidden sofa.	The dog **on the sofa** was asleep. or The dog **to watch for misbehavior** was asleep on the forbidden sofa. or The dog, **its tail dangling over the edge**, was asleep on the forbidden sofa.	The dog, **which was asleep on the forbidden sofa,** should be carefully watched for misbehavior.

Adjective Words: Adjectives describe people, places, objects, feelings, or activities.

Examples:

People: *erudite* professor, *whiny* kid, *svelte* model, *naive* rube

Places: *weird* room, *interstate* highway, *ghost* town, *huge* campus

Objects: *intricate* tattoo, *wedding* ring, *opaque* glass, *sleek* car

Feelings or ideas: *deep* joy, *strong* fear, *clear* memory, *funny* thought

Activities: *frantic* dancing, *thrilling* race, *brutal* exercise, *soft* caress

---

Adjective Phrases: There are four different adjective phrases.

One kind of adjective phrase, *a prepositional phrase that describes*, begins with a preposition: ***near** the tree,* ***above** the roof,* ***by** the arena,* ***in** the valley,* and so on. *Note:* Another kind of prepositional phrase (page 157) works like an adverb because it *tells how, when, where,* or *why* something happened.

Part One: Which underlined phrases are <u>adjective prepositional phrases</u> because they *describe* someone or something?

1. <u>In that very first moment</u>, when Houghton swished off the cloth, all Harrison had was a hunch.

   Malcolm Gladwell, *Blink*

2. Some other shepherd, <u>with a larger flock of sheep</u>, had arrived there before him and asked for her hand.

   Paulo Coelho, *The Alchemist*

3. <u>For food, a night's lodging, and the use of our piano</u>, he tuned it and gave Caroline and me free lessons.

   Katherine Paterson, *Jacob Have I Loved*

4. The apartment was small, <u>with slanting floors and irregular heat and an inoperable downstairs buzzer</u>.

   Barack Obama, *Dreams from My Father*

5. Government <u>of the people</u>, <u>by the people</u>, <u>for the people</u> shall not perish from the earth.

   Abraham Lincoln, the Gettysburg Address

A second kind of adjective phrase, *an infinitive phrase*, begins with the word *to* plus a verb: <u>*to tell*</u> *a story,* <u>*to surprise*</u> *my friend,* <u>*to write*</u> *well.* Such infinitive phrases describe someone or something. *Note:* Other infinitive phrases work like nouns (pages 43–47) or adverbs (pages 165–71), but they don't describe someone or something; they name something (noun infinitive) or *tell how, when, where, or why* something happened (adverb infinitive).

Part Two: Which underlined phrases are <u>adjective infinitive phrases</u> because they *describe* someone or something?

1. We felt an impulse <u>to sing, to break into a run, to snigger</u>.

   George Orwell, "A Hanging"

2. He began <u>to shiver</u>.

   Ray Bradbury, *The Martian Chronicles*

3. Beulah, <u>to prove her absolute power in the classroom</u>, ignored the teacher.

   Rosa Guy, *The Friends*

4. Mostly, it was a way <u>to unwind for a while with your closest friends</u>.

   Kazuo Ishiguro, *Never Let Me Go*

5. <u>To keep ourselves from going crazy from boredom</u>, we tried to think of word games.

   Barbara Kingsolver, *The Bean Trees*

A third kind of adjective phrase, *a participial phrase*, begins with an *ing* or *ed* word. Participial phrases are a descriptive link to someone or something mentioned elsewhere in the sentence:

Present Participial Phrase (ing)—Everywhere you stepped, little grasshoppers would fly up by the score, **making that snap they do like striking a match.** *(Describes the grasshoppers.)*

   Marilynne Robinson, *Gilead*

Past Participial Phrase (ed)—In front of him loomed the backdrop of high snow-covered mountains, **dressed in heavily wooded forests.** *(Describes the mountains.)*

   William P. Young, *The Shack*

Part Three: Find the participial phrase in each sentence below.

1. The singer, standing at the back of the crowd, was as poorly dressed as the doctor's daughter was well dressed.

   Toni Morrison, *Song of Solomon*

2. Curled in her burrow in the storeroom, Eliza began to die.

   Isabel Allende, *Daughter of Fortune*

3. Picking his way down a narrow gorge, Mortenson stepped off ice and onto solid ground for the first time in more than three months.

   Greg Mortenson and David Oliver Relin, *Three Cups of Tea*

4. Marlena and I stood perfectly still, stunned into silence.

   Sara Gruen, *Water for Elephants*

5. McTeague was a young giant, carrying his huge shock of blond hair six feet three inches from the ground.

   Frank Norris, *McTeague*

A fourth kind of adjective phrase, *an absolute phrase*, provides descriptive details about someone or something. An absolute phrase is <u>*almost*</u> a complete sentence. As a test, <u>you can make every absolute phrase into a sentence by adding **was** or **were**</u>.

Examples:

The man was watching me, **his eyes grey like the sea**.

   Tracy Chevalier, *Girl with the Pearl Earring*

   Test: His eyes [*were*] grey like the sea

Men, their caps pulled down, swung by.

   Katherine Mansfield, "The Voyage"

   Test: Their caps [*were*] pulled down.

Absolutes that function as adjectives <u>*always*</u> begin with a possessive pronoun: *my, his, her, its, our, their*. The pronoun can be visible (stated) or invisible (implied). *Note: Its* (no apostrophe) is a possessive pronoun; *it's* (apostrophe) is a contraction meaning *"it is."* Begin absolute phrases with *its*, not *it's*.

Visible Pronoun: A wild-eyed horse, **its bridle torn and dangling**, trotted frantically through the mounds of men, tossing its head, whinnying in panic. (*The pronoun* its *is visible before* bridle, *stated not implied.*)

   Lois Lowry, *The Giver*

Invisible Pronoun: **Gun still drawn**, he took a step forward when suddenly the bush behind him seemed to explode. *(The word* his *is invisible before* gun, *implied not stated.)*

William P. Young, *The Shack*

Part Four: Which underlined phrases are <u>absolute phrases</u> because they could be made into sentences by adding *was* or *were*?

1. <u>Their heads came up wildly</u> as spray blowed from their nostrils.

   Conrad Richter, "Early Marriage"

2. The fallen rider twitched once and lay motionless, <u>his legs bent at unnatural angles</u>.

   Khaled Hosseini, *The Kite Runner*

3. <u>His features are strong</u>, but they lack the nice symmetry and proportion that break young girls' hearts.

   Kenneth Brower, *The Starship and the Canoe*

4. In that dim light, in the corner of the couch, barely blinking, not reading, radio silent, the television rarely on, she was an old spider, stuck to <u>her own web</u>.

   Roya Hakakian, *Journey from the Land of No*

5. I came upon a sight that made my knees buckle, <u>my breath freezing as I fell to the familiar body</u>.

   Amelia Atwater-Rhodes, *Hawksong*

Adjective Clauses: Most adjective clauses begin with one of these words—*who, whose, which, where*. They are sentence parts (<u>not</u> complete sentences) containing a subject (underlined <u>once</u>) and a predicate (underlined <u>twice</u>).

Who: Over lunch, Beattie talked about her older sister, **<u>who</u> <u>was addicted to the shopping network.</u>**

Sue Miller, *While I Was Gone*

Whose: Sometimes one finds in fossil stones the imprint of a leaf, **<u>whose outlines</u> <u>remind us how detailed, vibrant, and alive are the things of this earth that perish</u>**.

Diane Ackerman, *A Natural History of the Senses*

Which: His hair, **which was almost exactly like his mother's in color and quality**, was a little sun-bleached on top.

J. D. Salinger, "The Laughing Man"

Where: My brother Buckley went on a day-trip to the Museum of Natural History in New York, **where he fell in love with the huge skeletons on display**.

Alice Sebold, *The Lovely Bones*

Part Five: Find the adjective clause in each sentence below.

1. More than midway down the block, Janet Gordon, who had been one of Clara's best friends, came out and picked up the baby.

   Edward P. Jones, *Lost in the City*

2. In the woods, after they had gone a long way from the road, Jesse stopped in an opening among the trees, where a clearing, overgrown with small bushes, ran up from the creek.

   Sherwood Anderson, *Winesburg, Ohio*

3. Everyone except Jon, whose nickname was Chuck, talked incessantly.

   Maya Angelou, *The Heart of a Woman*

4. Kinko spent the first few hours using bits of beef jerky to teach Queenie the elephant, who had apparently recovered from her diarrhea, to walk on her hind legs.

   Sara Gruen, *Water for Elephants*

5. At midmorning, the sailors had caught an enormous shark, which died on deck, thrashing wickedly in its death throes, while no one dared go near enough to club it.

   Isabel Allende, *Daughter of Fortune*

Review

Directions: For sentences with **boldfaced** *adjective tools*, exchange one of your own for the author's. For sentences with *deleted adjective tools*, expand the sentence by adding one of your own at the caret (^).

EXAMPLE OF EXCHANGING ———————————————————

Author's: I took off my bandanna, **shaking the dust from my hair.**

> Joyce Weatherford, *Heart of the Beast*

Yours: I took off my bandanna, **preferring the way my hair looked without it.**

EXAMPLE OF EXPANDING ———————————————————

Author's Sentence with Deleted Tool: She had a happy, helpless expression on her face, **which ^.**

Your Added Tool: She had a happy, helpless expression on her face, **which looked much healthier than it had the day before.**

Original Sentence: She had a happy, helpless expression on her face, **which was flushed and hot.**

> Jeffrey Eugenides, *Middlesex*

Adjective Words: Exchange the first five. Expand the next five.

1. **Awake,** listening to one lonely dog bark in the distance, Wesley began to shiver.

   > Stephen King, *UR*

2. I had seen her at home, **alone,** in her house gown, in the thirty-five-watt gloom of the living room lamp.

   > Roya Hakakian, *Journey from the Land of No*

3. Later, to his relief, when he found the courage to check with his fingers, each tooth was still there, **intact.**

   > Markus Zusak, *The Book Thief*

4. The face of the corpse was very truculent, **grey** and **massive**, with black cavernous nostrils and circled by a scanty white fur.

    James Joyce, *Dubliners*

5. She is a robust blonde, perhaps in her forties, **petite** yet **powerful**.

    Perri Knize, *A Piano Odyssey*

6. ^, brimming with the irrepressible joy of his own intelligence, Sandy Glass smiled most when he was angry.

    Allegra Goodman, *Intuition*

7. Jack's red hair, ^, had started falling out.

    Stephen King, *Everything's Eventual*

8. ^, we drifted away, huddling in makeshift shelters, lost for good.

    Keith Donohue, *The Stolen Child*

9. At six foot two, he was built like an oak, ^ and ^.

    Alex Kotlowitz, *Never a City So Real*

10. Then there was the unforgettable gun, ^ and ^.

    Jhumpa Lahiri, *Unaccustomed Earth*

Adjective Phrases: Exchange the first five. Expand the next five.

1. They sat burrowed into the sides of the heavily wooded mountain, **peering into their rifle scopes.**

    James McBride, *Miracle at St. Anna*

2. **Curled in her burrow in the storeroom**, Eliza began to die.

    Isabel Allende, *Daughter of Fortune*

3. The spiders lie on their sides, translucent and ragged, **their legs drying in knots.**

    Annie Dillard, "Death of a Moth"

4. He didn't want to think about the possibility that some other shepherd, **with a larger flock of sheep**, had arrived there before him and asked for her hand.

    Paulo Coelho, *The Alchemist*

5. A writer's work is a constant struggle **to get the right word in the right place**.

   Paul Roberts, "How to Say Nothing in Five Hundred Words"

6. The elephant swung her trunk across the ground in front of her huge body, fanning ^.

   Sara Gruen, *Water for Elephants*

7. The fallen rider twitched once and lay motionless, his ^.

   Khaled Hosseini, *The Kite Runner*

8. The sign of intelligence in reading is the ability to ^.

   Mortimer Adler, "How to Mark a Book"

9. On her monthly visits, dressed ^, she forced smiles and held her tongue.

   Maya Angelou, *The Heart of a Woman*

10. Late in the afternoon, his canary bird, in ^, began to sing.

    Frank Norris, *McTeague*

Adjective Clauses: Exchange the first five. Expand the next five.

1. Louise, **whose mind was filled with thoughts of John Hardy**, tried to make talk, but the country boy was embarrassed and would say nothing.

   Sherwood Anderson, *Winesburg, Ohio*

2. We were going to live in the Old Gatehouse, **where generations of Porters before us had lived**.

   Joanne Harris, *Gentlemen and Players*

3. The granddaughter, **who barely looked at Anil after the first shaking of hands**, was speaking loudly.

   Michael Ondaatje, *Anil's Ghost*

4. They recalled the chicken salad LeRoy brought to the Labor Day potluck picnic, **which had been sitting in the rear window of his car for a few hours**, and the waves of propulsive vomiting it caused.

   Garrison Keillor, *Pontoon*

5. Seventeenth century European women and men sometimes wore beauty patches in the shape of hearts, suns, moons, and stars, applying them to their breasts and faces, to draw an admirer's eye away from any imperfections, **which, in that era, too often included smallpox scars.**

   Diane Ackerman, "The Face of Beauty"

6. We went out and blew the better part of two weeks' pay for a handwoven Persian rug, which ^.

   John Grogan, *Marley & Me*

7. I looked at my mother, who ^.

   Tracy Chevalier, *Girl with the Pearl Earring*

8. Over the portals of the Palace of the World Council, there are words cut in the marble, which ^.

   Ayn Rand, *Anthem*

9. The orchards, whose ^, suddenly bloomed, all at once.

   Barbara Kingsolver, *Animal Dreams*

10. He was quite tanned, and his hair, which ^ , was a little sun-bleached on top.

    J. D. Salinger, "The Laughing Man"

---

*"I've always loved the flirtatious tango of consonants and vowels, the sturdy dependability of nouns and capricious whimsy of verbs, the strutting pageantry of the **adjective** and the flitting evanescence of the adverb, all kept safe and orderly by those reliable little policemen—punctuation marks. Wow! Think I got my ass kicked in high school?"*
—Dennis Miller, American comedian

In the next pages, you'll learn and practice how authors use each of the tools in the adjective group to build their sentences, and how you can use them, too.

Opening and Delayed Adjectives

In each pair, the second sentence has an adjective in the opener, S-V split, or closer position. Notice how its position adds emphasis to the description.

1a. He failed to see the main trail fork down to the river.

1b. **Lost in contemplation of the greenery,** he failed to see the main trail fork down to the river. *(opening adjective)*

> Greg Mortenson and David Oliver Relin, *Three Cups of Tea*

2a. His teeth were still intact.

2b. His teeth, **strong enough to shatter walnuts,** were still intact. *(S-V split adjective—between a subject and verb)*

> Truman Capote, *In Cold Blood*

3a. I had seen her at home.

3b. I had seen her at home, **alone in her house gown in the thirty-five-watt gloom of the living room lamp.** *(closer adjective)*

> Roya Hakakian, *Journey from the Land of No*

WHAT IS AN OPENING ADJECTIVE? *It's an adjective word or phrase in the opener position of a sentence. It always* precedes *what is described.*

Number: Sentences can contain either single or multiple opening adjectives:

*Single—***Wordless,** we split up.

> Annie Dillard, *An American Childhood*

*Multiple—***Dizzy** and **sick to his stomach,** he really felt as if the whole car were moving beneath him.

> Michael Crichton, *Jurassic Park*

WHAT IS A DELAYED ADJECTIVE? *It's an adjective word or phrase in the S-V split or closer position of a sentence. It always* follows *what is described.*

Number: Sentences can contain either single or multiple delayed adjectives:

Single—His chin, **<u>bristly</u> with sparse whiskers**, rested on the back of one hand. *(S-V split)*

> Annie Dillard, *An American Childhood*

Multiple—He was an elderly man, **<u>thin</u>** and **<u>frail</u>**. *(closer)*

> Michael Crichton, *Jurassic Park*

Positions:

S-V split: Brian, **<u>afraid</u> that Dad might toss Juju out the window**, held the dog tight.

> Jeannette Walls, *The Glass Castle*

Closer: The punks at the new Harvard Square T stop had tramped off, **<u>bright</u> as winter cardinals with their purple tufted hair and orange Mohawks.**

> Allegra Goodman, *Intuition*

PRACTICE 1: MATCHING

Match the adjective with the sentence. Write out each sentence, underlining the opening or delayed adjective.

Sentences:

1. ^, she stepped daintily across the clearing and struck me hard across the face.

   > Mildred D. Taylor, *Roll of Thunder, Hear My Cry*

2. Milk, ^, attracted every small flying thing from gnats to grasshoppers.

   > Edward Abbey, "Aravaipa Canyon"

3. Our father was younger than the landlord, ^.

   > James Baldwin, *Tell Me How Long the Train's Been Gone*

Opening or Delayed Adjectives:

a. alive

b. leaner, stronger, and bigger

c. red with anger

4. ^, the elephant was worth at least a hundred pounds, but dead, he would only be worth the value of his tusks, five pounds, possibly.

    George Orwell, "Shooting an Elephant"

    d. bright and pulsing like a boil

5. The anger was right out in the open now, ^.

    Stephen King, *Bag of Bones*

    e. sticky and sour on her dress

PRACTICE 2: UNSCRAMBLING

Rearrange the scrambled list of sentence parts to match the structure of the model. Next, write an imitation of the model. Finally, identify the *opening adjectives* in the model and your imitation.

MODEL: Awake in his bed, listening to one lonely dog bark in the distance, Wesley began to shiver.

    Stephen King, *UR*

  a. alert from his Espresso
  b. Daniel
  c. thinking about an attractive proposition suggested by his boss
  d. started to scheme

PRACTICE 3: COMBINING

Combine the list of sentences into just one sentence that imitates the structure of the model. Next, write an imitation of the model. Finally, identify the *delayed adjectives* in the model and your imitation.

MODEL: After she kicked Uncle Jack out of the house, she looked even better, happier, looser, janglier, jaunty.

    Garrison Keillor, *Pontoon*

  a. Something happened when he sent the children to boarding school.
  b. Then, he appeared bereft.
  c. He also seemed lonelier.

    d. He also acted moodier.

    e. He also looked gloomier.

    f. He also was adrift.

PRACTICE 4: IMITATING

Write an imitation of each model sentence so good that nobody can tell yours from the author's.

Models and Sample Imitations:

1. Curious, he exited the bathroom and poked his head through the doorway of the kitchen.

              William P. Young, *The Shack*

Sample: Alone, she walked the beach and collected sea shells along the edge of the surf.

2. Eager to feed mankind, Mother rushed to the door with a lunchbox.

              Roya Hakakian, *Journey from the Land of No*

Sample: Unable to eat breakfast, Samantha sidled out of the kitchen with a smirk.

3. The door swung wide then, and an elderly woman, frail and toothless, stepped out.

              Mildred D. Taylor, *Roll of Thunder, Hear My Cry*

Sample: The sun came up brightly, and a timid rabbit, hungry and alone, scampered over.

PRACTICE 5: EXCHANGING

To practice writing good opening or delayed adjectives, exchange one of yours for the author's. Try to make yours as good as—maybe even better than—the author's.

Example:

Author's: Tom, looking down toward the tent, saw his mother, **heavy** and **slow with weariness**, build a little trash fire and put the cooking pots over the flame.

              John Steinbeck, *The Grapes of Wrath*

Yours: Tom, looking down toward the tent, saw his mother, **desperate** but **creative with solutions**, build a little trash fire and put the cooking pots over the flame.

1. Brian, **afraid that Dad might toss Juju out the window**, held the dog tight.

    Jeannette Walls, *The Glass Castle*

2. The Parker-Morris Building will go over, all one hundred and ninety-one floors, **slow as a tree falling in the forest**.

    Chuck Palahniuk, *Fight Club*

3. This boy looked a couple of years younger than I was, **too young to deserve this horror, too young to die**.

    Amelia Atwater-Rhodes, *Hawksong*

PRACTICE 6: EXPANDING

Partner with the author by creating an adjective word or phrase at the caret (^).

1. They carried their shoes down the hall and stopped at the top landing where they could see into their father's room, ^.

    Kent Haruf, *Plainsong*

2. He was only aware that the right side of his face was suddenly as hot as a furnace, and that blood, ^, ^, and ^, was pouring down the side of his neck.

    Stephen King, *Needful Things*

3. ^, ^, and ^, the drowning bulldog swam a round or two before he went down.

    Wallace Stegner, *Crossing to Safety*

COMPOSITION: Travel Essay

ASSIGNMENT: Opening and delayed adjectives have descriptive power because their unusual placement is a spotlight. Find a picture of an unusual place—bizarre, spiritual, quirky, romantic, scary, serene, lush, offbeat, glamorous, exotic, and so on. Pretend you are a journalist hired to cover that place for the travel section of a print or electronic publication: newspaper, magazine, or website.

Somewhere within your description, include five *adjective phrases from the list below*, excerpts from sentences by authors. Build a sentence around the phrase, using the adjective phrase in the opening or delayed position. Also include *five adjective phrases of your own* for other sentences in the description, with some as opening adjectives and some as delayed adjectives. Aim for approximately 250 words to complete your report of the place.

Adjective Phrases:

1. black in color
   Cormac McCarthy. *No Country for Old Men*

2. rich in ideas and beauty
   Mortimer Adler, "How to Mark a Book"

3. scarcely discernable from the surrounding city lights
   Kim Harrison, *Every Which Way but Dead*

4. raucous as crows
   Pat Conroy, *My Losing Season*

5. leafless and almost black
   Louise Erdrich, *The Master Butchers Singing Club*

6. lit by the orange glow of a fire in the wintertime
   Khaled Hosseini, *The Kite Runner*

7. solemn and truculent in death
   James Joyce, *Dubliners*

8. lost for good
   Keith Donohue, *The Stolen Child*

9. out of sight
   Michael Ondaatje, *Anil's Ghost*

10. very lovely
    Katherine Mansfield, "Bliss"

11. beautiful, sensuous, gifted, good-natured beyond belief
    Ian McEwan, *On Chesil Beach*

12. silent, separate, and pleasantly mysterious
    Toni Morrison, *The Bluest Eye*

13. treeless and barren
    Barack Obama, *Dreams from My Father*

14. mauve and pink
    Joyce Weatherford, *Heart of the Beast*

15. grey and massive

   James Joyce, *Dubliners*

16. happier, looser, janglier, jaunty

   Garrison Keillor, *Pontoon*

17. thin and frail beyond belief,
   but wiry, indomitable

   Joan Aiken, "Searching for Summer"

18. glad to go in

   James Joyce, *Portrait of the Artist as a Young Man*

---

*"Adjectives you can do
anything with."*
—Lewis Carroll, *Through the Looking Glass*

Participial Phrase

In each pair, the second sentence has a participial phrase. Notice how it makes the sentence more visual.

1a. Mouzafer crouched in the cave.

1b. Mouzafer crouched in the cave, **blowing violently on the sagebrush he'd lit with a flint until it bloomed into flame.** *(Participial phrase describes Mouzafer's actions in the cave.)*

> Greg Mortenson and David Oliver Relin, *Three Cups of Tea*

2a. Dad steered the car through the dark.

2b. Dad steered the car through the dark, **driving slowly so as not to alert anyone in the trailer park that we were doing the skedaddle.** *(Participial phrase describes how Dad drove.)*

> Jeannette Walls, *The Glass Castle*

3a. His wife tensed and cried out, and the baby moved in the birth canal.

3b. His wife tensed and cried out, and the baby moved in the birth canal, **bursting the amniotic sac.** *(Participial phrase describes what happened when the baby moved.)*

> Kim Edwards, *The Memory Keeper's Daughter*

WHAT IS A PARTICIPIAL PHRASE? *It's a verbal ending in* ing *or* ed *used to describe.* A verbal is a verb that also functions like another part of speech. Participles show action, so they act like verbs, but they also describe, so they act like adjectives.

Present participles always end in *ing*. Unlike *ing* verbs, which cannot be removed from a sentence, participles are removable.

Verb (not removable): He was **blowing violently on the sagebrush he'd lit.**

If *blowing violently on the sagebrush he'd lit* were removed, the sentence would be ruined:

He was (incomplete sentence)

Present Participle (removable): Mouzafer crouched in the cave, **blowing violently on the sagebrush he'd lit.**

> Greg Mortenson and David Oliver Relin, *Three Cups of Tea*

If *blowing violently on the sagebrush he'd lit* were removed, the sentence would *not* be ruined:

Mouzafer crouched in the cave. (complete sentence)

Difference Between Present Participles and Gerunds—Like present participles, gerunds (page 35) are verbals that also end in *ing*, but it's easy to tell the difference between gerunds and present participles. Present participles are removable sentence parts; gerunds are not. *In each pair, the first contains a present participle, and the second contains a gerund.* Notice that only the present participles can be removed.

1a. *Feeling so much better after the nap*, Gunster dressed and went out.

1b. *Feeling so much better after the nap* relieved Gunster.

2a. Ralston, *going down the staircase backward*, was very unsteady.

2b. The cause of Ralston's fall was *going down the staircase backward*.

3a. The damaged plane landed poorly, *skidding left and right with sparks flying everywhere.*

3b. The captain during touchdown worried about *skidding left and right with sparks flying everywhere.*

Past participles usually end in *ed*. Unlike *ed* verbs, which cannot be removed from a sentence, past participles are removable. *Note:* Most past participles end in *ed*; others—by far the minority—end in *en* (*forgiven*) or end irregularly (*sung*). This worktext treats only the most common—those with *ed*—because once you learn the *ed* participles, you will intuit and use the others.

Verb (not removable): A wide pink ribbon was **tied in back with a bow**.

If *tied in back with a bow* were removed, the sentence would be ruined:

A wide pink ribbon was (incomplete sentence)

Past Participle (removable): Around her waist was a wide pink ribbon, **tied in back with a bow.**

Bill Brittain, *The Wish Giver*

If *tied in back with a bow* were removed, the sentence would <u>not</u> be ruined: *Around her waist was a wide pink ribbon.* (complete sentence)

Good writers sometimes use *multiple* participles within the same sentence.

Present participles: Sometimes at night, I wished I could go back to prowl the forests, **spooking sleeping birds from their roosts, stealing clothes from clotheslines,** and **making merry rather than enduring page after page of homework.** *(three)*

Keith Donohue, *The Stolen Child*

Past participles: **Hated by the Federalists** and **suspected by the Republicans,** John Quincy Adams returned to private life. *(two)*

John F. Kennedy, *Profiles in Courage*

Position: Participial phrases occur in three positions:

Present Participial Phrases

Opener—**Picking his way down a narrow gorge,** Mortenson stepped off ice and onto solid ground for the first time in more than three months.

Greg Mortenson and David Oliver Relin, *Three Cups of Tea*

S-V split—The singer, **standing at the back of the crowd,** was as poorly dressed as the doctor's daughter was well dressed.

Toni Morrison, *Song of Solomon*

Closer—He struggled with poverty, **working sixteen hours a day for $11 a month.**

Stephen E. Ambrose, *Nothing Like It in the World*

Past Participial Phrases

Opener—**Dismayed at how difficult it was to carry a heavy cello a half mile to school,** I switched to the more portable flute.

Perri Knize, *A Piano Odyssey*

S-V split—One structure, **rejected at first as a monstrosity,** became the world fair's emblem, a machine so huge and terrifying that it instantly eclipsed the tower of Alexandre Eiffel that had so wounded America's pride.

Eric Larson, *The Devil in the White City*

Closer—Marlena and I stood perfectly still, **stunned into silence.**

Marilynne Robinson, *Gilead*

Adjective Group: The Describing Tools

PRACTICE 1: MATCHING

Match the participial phrase with the sentence. Write out each sentence, underlining each participial phrase.

Sentences:

1. In the livid light of the fluorescent tube over the kitchen sink, he made out a slender young man of about his own age, ^ .

   Michael Chabon, *The Amazing Adventures of Kavalier & Clay*

2. The hangman, ^, produced a small cotton bag like a flour bag and drew it down over the prisoner's face.

   George Orwell, "A Hanging"

3. We wandered about the stock exhibit, ^.

   Dorothy Canfield Fisher, "The Heyday of the Blood"

4. The stadium itself, two white concrete banks of seats, was as powerful and alien to me as an Aztec ruin, ^.

   John Knowles, *A Separate Peace*

5. For two nights and days, ^, the dog neither ate nor drank.

   Jack London, *The Call of the Wild*

Participial Phrases:

a. filled with the traces of vanished rites, of supreme emotions and supreme tragedies

b. imprisoned in his crate

c. gazing at the monstrous oxen and hanging over the railings where the prize pigs loved to scratch their backs

d. slumped like a question mark against the door frame

e. standing still on the gallows

PRACTICE 2: UNSCRAMBLING

Rearrange the scrambled list of sentence parts to match the structure of the model. Next, write an imitation of the model. Finally, identify the participial phrases in the model and your imitation.

MODEL: The sudden flood of light, pouring in on his half sleep, brought him leaping out of bed, braced for a new concussion.

John Hersey, *Hiroshima*

a. pounding down on the bedroom skylight
b. concerned about heavy water damage
c. got her thinking about the seedlings
d. the loud sound of raindrops

PRACTICE 3: COMBINING

Combine the list of sentences into just one sentence that imitates the structure of the model. Next, write an imitation of the model. Finally, identify the participial phrases in the model and your imitation.

MODEL: Sammy peered over his mother, trying to get a better look at poor Josef Kavalier in his baggy tweed suit.

Michael Chabon, *The Amazing Adventures of Kavalier & Clay*

a. The puppy leaped from my arms.
b. It was wanting to join the other pups.
c. The other pups were in the water from the hose.
d. The hose was in our neighbor's yard.

PRACTICE 4: IMITATING

Write an imitation of each model sentence so good that nobody can tell yours from the author's.

Models and Sample Imitations:

1. Weeping, shuddering, he sat on the edge of the bed.

Lois Lowry, *The Giver*

Sample: Pacing, waiting, he wondered about the results of his test.

2. The roads were terrible, swamped in dust where they were traveled and baked into ruts where they were not.

> Marilynne Robinson, *Gilead*

Sample: The ants were alarmed, frenzied with activity when they were revealed and buried under stones when they were not.

3. Leaning against the wall in the hall downstairs near the cloak-stand was a coffin-lid, covered with cloth of gold, ornamented with gold cords and tassels.

> Leo Tolstoy, "The Death of Ivan Ilyich"

Sample: Standing on the rug in the closet upstairs over the old kitchen was a suitcase, battered by years of use, dented with pock marks and scrapes.

PRACTICE 5: EXCHANGING

To practice writing good participial phrases, exchange one of yours for the author's. Try to make yours as good as—maybe even better than—the author's.

Example:

Author's: Ethan, **alerted now for signs of the wonderful in his daughter**, was struck by the strange fact that she was making conversation.

> John Updike, "Man and Daughter in the Cold"

Yours: Ethan, **amazed by the woman's sudden return to sobriety**, was struck by the strange fact that she was making conversation.

---

1. That night at dinner Bobby looked across the table at his sister with new eyes, **filled with awe and admiration.**

> Fannie Flag, *Standing in the Rainbow*

2. **Bleeding profusely but without his supply of eagles' blood**, he had never been closer to death.

> J. D. Salinger, "The Laughing Man"

3. He, **sensing a new and strange and quite terrified note in all this the moment he read it**, at once looked over his shoulder at her.

> Theodore Dreiser, *An American Tragedy*

PRACTICE 6: EXPANDING

Partner with the author by creating a participial phrase at the caret (^).

1. The rain, ^, bounced in the wet street.

> Wallace Stegner, *Crossing to Safety*

2. ^, she led me around the room in an impromptu waltz.

> Judith Ortiz Cofer, *Silent Dancing*

3. ^, ^, we worked all morning in opposite parts of the woods.

> Truman Capote, *The Grass Harp*

COMPOSITION: Action Paragraph

ASSIGNMENT: Participial phrases provide descriptive layering, creating vivid mental films of action. Below are two paragraphs narrating a long touchdown run by a football player nicknamed "Darling." In the first version, all participial phrases are removed. In the second version, those phrases—60 percent of the paragraph—are restored.

Find and use a picture or an electronic image showing any action—in sports, entertainment, news, and so on.

Write two paragraphs: first, a skeleton paragraph without participial phrases, telling only what happened; next, an expanded version with lots of participial phrases like the original paragraph, narrating mainly <u>through present participial phrases</u> the action shown.

Skeleton Paragraph without Participial Phrases

(1) The pass was high and wide and Darling jumped for it. (2) The center floated by. (3) He had ten yards in the clear and picked up speed. (4) He smiled a little to himself as he ran. (5) His knees and his hips kept moving him down the field. (6) The first halfback came at him, and he fed him his leg, then swung at the last moment, took the shock of the man's shoulder without breaking stride, and ran through him. (7) There was only the safety man now. (8) Darling tucked the ball in, spurted at him. *(95 words)*

Expanded Paragraph with Participial Phrases (adapted)

(1) The pass was high and wide and Darling jumped for it, **feeling it slap flatly against his hands as he shook his hips to throw off the halfback who was diving at him.** (2) The center floated by, **brushing Darling's knee as Darling picked his feet up high and delicately ran over a blocker and an opposing linesman**

in a jumble on the ground near the scrimmage line. (3) He had ten yards in the clear and picked up speed, **breathing easily, feeling his thigh pads rising and falling against his legs, listening to the sound of cleats behind him, pulling away from them, watching the other backs heading him off toward the side-line.** (4) He smiled a little to himself as he ran, **holding the ball lightly in front of him with his two hands.** (5) His knees, **pumping high,** and his hips, **twisting in the almost girlish run of a back in a broken field,** kept moving him down the field. (6) The first halfback came at him, and he fed him his leg, then swung at the last moment, took the shock of the man's shoulder without breaking stride, and ran through him. (7) There was only the safety man now, **coming warily at him with his arms crooked and his hands spread.** (8) Darling tucked the ball in, spurted at him, **driving hard, hurling himself along with his legs pounding and knees high and all two hundred pounds bunched into controlled attack.**
(239 words)

Irwin Shaw, "The Eighty-Yard Run"

Analyze the original paragraph:

How many participial phrases are in the paragraph?

What position are they all in—*opener, S-V split, or closer?*

How long are they on average—*short, medium, or long?*

How many sentences contain present participial phrases?

Process:

- First write a skeleton paragraph without participial phrases.

- Begin your paragraph by identifying the event you'll narrate.

- Narrate the event by telling what happened first, next, next, and so on.

- Expand the skeleton paragraph by adding participial phrases.

- End with a memorable sentence.

"Having imagination it takes you an hour to write a paragraph that if you were unimaginative would take you only a minute."
—Franklin Pierce Adams

Prepositional Phrase

In each pair, the second sentence has a prepositional phrase. Notice how it adds helpful information.

1a. She was a woman.

1b. She was a woman **with a broom or a dustpan or a washrag or a mixing spoon in her hand.** *(Describes the woman.)*

> Ray Bradbury, "Good-bye, Grandma"

2a. The house was too big for her father now.

2b. The house, **with the rooms her mother had decorated and the bed in which she liked to sit up doing crossword puzzles and the stove on which she'd cooked**, was too big for her father now. *(Describes what kind of house was too big.)*

> Jhumpa Lahiri, *Unaccustomed Earth*

3a. The snow was falling lightly, and I was breathing through my nose until it was running so much that I had to open my mouth.

3b. The snow was falling lightly, **like a flurry of small hands**, and I was breathing through my nose until it was running so much that I had to open my mouth. *(Describes what the snow resembled.)*

> Alice Sebold, *The Lovely Bones*

WHAT IS A PREPOSITIONAL PHRASE? *A preposition is any word that will fit in this blank:* **It was _____ the box.** *about the box, at the box, beyond the box, from the box, near the box, over the box, under the box, inside the box, outside the box, by the box, and so on.* Some prepositional phrases function like adjectives because they describe a noun. These phrases usually answer this question: What kind?

Examples:

1. Doors opened to him because of his skill **with cards and dice.** *(Tells what kind of skill.)*

> Isabel Allende, *Daughter of Fortune*

2. Government **of the people, by the people, for the people** shall not perish from the earth. *(Tells what kind of government won't perish.)*

> Abraham Lincoln, the Gettysburg Address

Note: See pages 157–63 for prepositional phrases that function like adverbs.

Adjective Group: The Describing Tools

Number: Sentences can contain either single, connected, or multiple prepositional phrases.

Single—The kids were lean and hard, **with callused hands and feet.**

> Jeannette Walls, *The Glass Castle*

Connected—This was Chicago, **on the eve of the greatest fair in history.** *(three connected prepositional phrases: **on the eve** and **of the greatest fair** and **in history**)*

> Eric Larson, *The Devil in the White City*

Multiple—**In 1959, at twenty-three**, my father arrived at the University of Hawaii as that institution's first African student. *(multiple prepositional phrases: **in 1959** and **at twenty-three**)*

> Barack Obama, *Dreams from My Father*

Position: Prepositional phrases occur in three positions:

Opener—**Like a furloughed captive**, Nazila wanted to store as much joy as fast as she could.

> Roya Hakakian, *Journey from the Land of No*

S-V split—Mom, **in an unnaturally calm voice**, explained what had happened and asked if we could please have a ride to the hospital.

> Jeannette Walls, *The Glass Castle*

Closer—He's a lanky, athletic man of thirty-nine, **with a cherubic face and a mop of curly hair.**

> Perri Knize, *A Piano Odyssey*

PRACTICE 1: MATCHING

Match the prepositional phrase with the sentence. Write out each sentence, underlining the prepositional phrase.

Sentences:

1. ^, he thought he had a novel in him somewhere and would write it someday.

> Stephen King, *UR*

Prepositional Phrases:

a. in fixtures that combined gas and electricity

2. Pressure against the body, ^, causes a tarantula to move off slowly for a short distance.

> Alexander Petrunkevitch, "The Spider and the Wasp"

b. in every variety of dress, from the Elizabethan knight to the buck of the Regency

3. A dim line of portraits of ancestors, ^, stared down upon us and daunted us by their silent company.

> Sir Arthur Conan Doyle, *The Hound of the Baskervilles*

c. like all instructors of English

4. Electric bulbs, ^, were just beginning to light the newest buildings.

> Eric Larson, *The Devil in the White City*

d. by a finger or the end of a pencil

5. It had been an excellent pregnancy, ^.

> Kim Edwards, *The Memory Keeper's Daughter*

e. without medical restrictions

PRACTICE 2: UNSCRAMBLING

Rearrange the scrambled list of sentence parts to match the structure of the model. Next, write an imitation of the model. Finally, identify prepositional phrases in the model and your imitation.

MODEL: In the distance, across the lake, a truck lumbered around a corner on the hill.

> Khaled Hosseini, *The Kite Runner*

    a. the pills sat
    b. on a plate with a crack
    c. in the kitchen
    d. with some water

PRACTICE 3: COMBINING

Combine the list of sentences into just one sentence that imitates the structure of the model. Next, write an imitation of the model. Finally, identify prepositional phrases in the model and your imitation.

MODEL: Both farms were located in gorgeous natural settings that attract tourists, with backdrops of high snow-capped mountains drained by streams teeming with fish.

Jared Diamond, *Collapse*

    a. One woman was dressed in bright, vivid colors that flattered her.
    b. She was dressed with accents of cheerful costume jewelry.
    c. The jewelry was highlighted by a bracelet.
    d. The bracelet was dazzling with rhinestones.

PRACTICE 4: IMITATING

Write an imitation of each model sentence so good that nobody can tell yours from the author's.

Models and Sample Imitations:

1. Ima Dean, with a huge bag of yellow and red wrapped candies, was sitting on the floor, delving into it, making one big pile and three smaller ones.

Bill and Vera Cleaver, *Where the Lilies Bloom*

Sample: Brittany, in an unmade bed of tussled and comfortable Egyptian sheets, was looking at the magazine, paging through it, noting the best illustrations and some enticing ads.

2. Her husband was boyishly handsome, with generous, curling brown-blond hair, a whittled marathoner's body, sharply attractive cheekbones.

Jhumpa Lahiri, *Unaccustomed Earth*

Sample: Their garden was lavishly beautiful, with colorful, seasonal eye-catching displays, an enchanting rock garden, subtly fragrant scents.

3. Nestled at the top of a brown stony hill above the modern Cretan village of Lentas are the ruins of an ancient temple to the Greek god Asclepius, the Greek god of healing.

Esther M. Sternberg, *The Balance Within*

Sample: Situated on 5th Avenue within the sophisticated shopping area of New York is an ice-skating rink with a statue in gold of Atlas, a titan in mythology.

PRACTICE 5: EXCHANGING

To practice writing good prepositional phrases, exchange one of yours for the author's. Try to make yours as good as—maybe even better than—the author's.

Example:

Author's: The class buildings, **with their backs practically against the forest wall**, formed a semicircle facing a small one-room church at the opposite end of the compound.

Mildred D. Taylor, *Roll of Thunder, Hear My Cry*

Yours: The class buildings, **near the memorial tower in honor of the founder of the college**, formed a semicircle facing a small one-room church at the opposite end of the compound.

1. People **from all over the world** have passed through this village.

Paulo Coelho, *The Alchemist*

2. **At the crossroads over the bridge**, he met two friends and the three of them walked to school together, making ridiculous strides and being rather silly.

John Steinbeck, *The Red Pony*

3. **On this mound, among the grasses and the plants**, stood Rontu.

Scott O'Dell, *Island of the Blue Dolphins*

PRACTICE 6: EXPANDING

Partner with the author by creating a prepositional phrase at the caret (^).

1. **Outside ^, in ^,** she could see a huge jagged slab of ice sticking up from the snow.

Susan Fromberg Schaeffer, *Time in Its Flight*

2. Somewhere **beyond ^, past ^, under ^,** a boy and a yearling ran side by side, and were gone forever.

Marjorie Kinnan Rawlings, *The Yearling*

3. Then he talked **of ^, of ^, of ^, of ^.**

James Hilton, *Goodbye, Mr. Chips*

COMPOSITION: Descriptive Paragraph

ASSIGNMENT: Skillful writers sometimes include consecutive prepositional phrases within a sentence. Sometimes, as in the sentences below, those phrases begin with the same word to magnify the description.

Write a sentence that includes <u>at least three consecutive prepositional phrases, each beginning with the same word</u>. After writing your sentence, include it as one of the sentences in a paragraph describing a scene or event. In addition to prepositional phrases, use other sentence-composing tools to enhance your paragraph.

1. They whisper many strange things, **<u>of</u> the towers which rose to the sky in those Unmentionable Times, <u>of</u> the wagons which moved without horses, and <u>of</u> the lights which burned without flame.**

   Ayn Rand, *Anthem*

2. Her mother would have stuck out, **<u>in</u> her brightly colored saris, <u>in</u> her dime-sized maroon bindi, <u>in</u> her jewels.**

   Jhumpa Lahiri, *Unaccustomed Earth*

3. There were a thousand people **<u>on</u> the ground, <u>on</u> the town hall steps, <u>on</u> the rooftops that surrounded the square.**

   Markus Zusak, *The Book Thief*

4. She taught us to be impolite in conversation **<u>about</u> sexual matters, <u>about</u> American history and famous heroes, <u>about</u> the distribution of wealth, <u>about</u> school, <u>about</u> everything.**

   Kurt Vonnegut, *Breakfast of Champions*

Process:

- Analyze why the authors of the examples arranged their phrases as they did.

- Plan for the most effective arrangement of your phrases by deciding which should come first, second, third, and so on.

- Develop the paragraph with additional sentences describing layers of details in the scene.

---

*"The rule which forbids ending a sentence with a preposition
is the kind of nonsense up with which I will not put."*
—Winston Churchill, British prime minister

Infinitive Phrase

In each pair, the second sentence has an adjective infinitive. Notice how it provides clarity and elaboration.

1a. Mrs. Myers barked the command.

1b. Mrs. Myers barked the command **to stand for the pledge of allegiance.** *(Adjective infinitive describes the command.)*
Katherine Paterson, Bridge to Terabithia

2a. Throughout their formative years, temptations were kept out of the way of the young people, so that their honesty could have every chance.

2b. Throughout their formative years, temptations were kept out of the way of the young people, so that their honesty could have every chance **to harden and solidify and become a part of their very bone.** *(Adjective infinitive describes the chance.)*
Mark Twain, "The Man That Corrupted Hadleyburg"

3a. There wasn't time.

3b. There wasn't time **to explain that Mac was a young, witty, macho cop who walked into the hospital with 32 pounds of attack equipment, looking as if he could single-handedly protect the whole city if not the entire state.** *(Adjective infinitive describes the time.)*
Barbara Huttmann, "A Crime of Compassion"

WHAT IS AN ADJECTIVE INFINITIVE PHRASE? *It's a phrase that <u>describes</u> something and that begins with* to *plus a verb: to sing, to read, to linger, to laugh, to sigh, to study, and so on.*

Infinitive phrases can describe something (like adjectives), or name something (like nouns), or explain something (like adverbs).

1. *Adjective infinitive*—The coach emphasized the need **to make it to the final round of the playoffs.** *The infinitive <u>describes</u> the need. Adjective infinitives answer the question "What kind?"*

2. *Noun infinitive*—**To make it to the final round of the playoffs** was the team's goal. *The infinitive <u>names</u> the team's goal. Noun infinitives answer the question "What?" (See pages 43–47.)*

115

3. *Adverb infinitive*—The team from Western High School worked overtime **to make it to the final round of the playoffs.** *The infinitive <u>explains why</u> the team worked overtime. Adverb infinitives answer the question "Why?"* (See pages 165–71.)

Number: Sentences can contain either single or multiple adjective infinitives:

Single—The desire **to write** grows with writing. *(Describes what kind of desire grows with writing.)*

Erasmus

Multiple—The beach is not the place **to work, to read, to write, or to think.** *(Describes four activities inappropriate for a beach.)*

Anne Morrow Lindbergh, *Gift from the Sea*

PRACTICE 1: MATCHING

Match the adjective infinitive with the sentence. Write out each sentence, underlining the adjective infinitive.

Sentences:

1. The sign of intelligence in reading is the ability ^.

    Mortimer Adler, "How to Mark a Book"

2. A child is a guest in the house, ^, since he or she belongs to God.

    J. D. Salinger, *Raise High the Roof Beam, Carpenters*

3. A writer's work is a constant struggle ^.

    Paul Roberts, "How to Say Nothing in Five Hundred Words"

4. Eating safely from dumpsters involves using the senses and common sense ^.

    Lars Eighner, "On Dumpster Diving"

Adjective Infinitives:

a. to evaluate the condition of the found materials

b. to ask what I wanted to know

c. to be loved and respected, never possessed

d. to read different things differently according to their worth

5. There were a million ways ^, and I chose the worst one.

   Christopher Paul Curtis, *Bud, Not Buddy*

e. to get the right word in the right place, a struggle to find that particular word that will convey meaning exactly, that will persuade or soothe or startle or amuse the reader

PRACTICE 2: UNSCRAMBLING

Rearrange the scrambled list of sentence parts to match the structure of the model. Next, write an imitation of the model. Finally, identify the infinitives in the model and your imitation.

MODEL: Carefully taking the burning match from his friend's fingertips, he set it in the bowl, and in short order we had a fire to toast our palms and fingertips.

   Keith Donohue, *The Stolen Child*

   a. he put it on the table
   b. to focus our minds and attention
   c. and after a while we had an occupation
   d. expertly constructing the intricate board
   e. for the mathematical game

PRACTICE 3: COMBINING

Combine the list of sentences into just one sentence that imitates the structure of the model. Next, write an imitation of the model. Finally, identify the adjective infinitives in the model and your imitation.

MODEL: Swearing silently, Smith rolled and tumbled downhill, clawing frantically with his hands, stabbing his fingers into the dirt in an effort to slow his descent.

   Robert Ludlum, *The Moscow Vector*

   a. Tanya was moving carefully.
   b. She hopped and skipped across the stream.
   c. She was balancing unsteadily with her arms.
   d. She was placing her feet on the rocks in an attempt to anchor her feet.

PRACTICE 4: IMITATING

Write an imitation of each model sentence so good that nobody can tell yours from the author's.

Models and Sample Imitations:

1. We felt an impulse to sing, to break into a run, to snigger.

   George Orwell, "A Hanging"

   Sample: We had the idea to partner, to try out a strategy, to win.

2. Igel, the eldest and leader of the band, took pains to explain the ways of the forest.

   Keith Donohue, *The Stolen Child*

   Sample: Shea, the youngest and baby of the family, made squeals to express her enjoyment of the puppy.

3. The urge to give up, to turn back toward the comfort and warmth of his fellow men, was almost overpowering.

   John Christopher, *The Guardians*

   Sample: His decision to move then, to jump high over the width and breadth of the barbed fence, was virtually instinctive.

PRACTICE 5: EXCHANGING

To practice writing good adjective infinitives, exchange one of yours for the author's. Try to make yours as good as—maybe even better than—the author's.

Example:

Author's: He had a weak point, although in other regards he was a man **to be respected and even feared**.

   Edgar Allan Poe, "The Cask of Amontillado"

Yours: He had a weak point, although in other regards he was a man **to be admired and certainly appreciated**.

1. There was a last load of lumber **to be hauled to the village**, and Jotham Powell, who did not work regularly for Ethan in winter, had come round to help with the job.

   Edith Wharton, *Ethan Frome*

2. The world is very different now, for man holds in his mortal hands the power **to abolish all forms of human poverty and all forms of human life.**

   John F. Kennedy, inaugural address

3. She had had the colossal courage **to wash her face, slap cold cream on it, and push back the cuticle around her nails.**

   Edna Ferber, *Buttered Side Down*

PRACTICE 6: EXPANDING

Partner with the author by creating an infinitive phrase at the caret (^).

1. By far the best way **to ^** is to lower yourself into a dumpster.

   Lars Eighner, "On Dumpster Diving"

2. There was usually a lot of junk mail and a few big envelopes for her mother, a pile **to ^**.

   Jostein Gaarder, *Sophie's World*

3. Soon after the opening, quite a number of students who evidently were worthy, but who were so poor that they did not have any money **to ^** began applying for admission.

   Booker T. Washington, *Up from Slavery: An Autobiography*

COMPOSITION: Advertisement

ASSIGNMENT: The adjective infinitive tool, like all sentence-composing tools, can be multiplied by using two or more in a series. Assume you are in the marketing department for tourism for a city. Your job is to write an ad to promote that city.

In the library or on the Internet, learn about desirable tourist attractions to promote your city.

Process:

Use this as a model for your ad, a passage from the King James version of the Bible (Ecclesiastes 3:1). It uses multiple adjective infinitives to describe different purposes of time:

To every thing there is a season, and a time to every purpose under the heaven:

A time to be born, and a time to die; a time to plant, and a time to pluck up that which is planted;

A time to kill, and a time to heal; a time to break down, and a time to build up;

A time to weep, and a time to laugh; a time to mourn, and a time to dance. . . .

<u>Fill in this template of adjective infinitive phrases</u> to create a persuasive advertisement for the city you are promoting:

In (NAME OF CITY) there is an attraction, and a place for every interest for visitors:

A place to ?, and a place to ?; a place to ?, and a place to ?;

A place to ?, and a place to ?; a place to ?, and a place to ?;

A place to ?, and a place to ?; a place to ?, and a place to ? . . .

"To produce a progression of drafts, each of which says more and says it more clearly, the writer has to develop a special kind of reading skill."
—Donald M. Murray, "The Maker's Eye: Revising Your Own Manuscripts"

Absolute Phrase

In each pair, the second sentence has an absolute phrase. Notice how it adds detail, elaboration, and style.

1a. She returned to her bench.

1b. She returned to her bench, **her face showing all the unhappiness that had suddenly overtaken her.** *(Absolute phrase describes her.)*

   Theodore Dreiser, *An American Tragedy*

2a. I saw the mouse vanish in the general direction of my apartment house.

2b. I saw the mouse vanish in the general direction of my apartment house, **his little body quivering with fear in the great open sun on the blazing concrete.** *(Absolute phrase describes the mouse.)*

   Loren Eiseley, "The Brown Wasps"

3a. Willa sat by herself.

3b. Willa sat by herself, **her high-necked flower-print dress looking out of place among the Levi's, denim skirts, and pearl-button shirts.** *(Absolute phrase describes Willa.)*

   Stephen King, *Just After Sunset*

WHAT IS AN ABSOLUTE PHRASE? *It's a phrase describing someone or something mentioned elsewhere in the same sentence.* An absolute phrase is <u>almost</u> a complete sentence. As a test, you can make every absolute phrase into a sentence by adding *was* or *were*.

Examples:

1. He hiked on along the ridge with his thumb hooked in the shoulder strap of the rifle, **his hat pushed back on his head.**

   Cormac McCarthy, *No Country for Old Men*

   Test: His hat [*was*] pushed back on his head.

2. Scores of workers had been hurt or killed in building the dream, **their families consigned to poverty.**

   Eric Larson, *The Devil in the White City*

   Test: Their families [*were*] consigned to poverty.

Absolutes that function as adjectives *always* begin with a possessive pronoun: *my, his, her, its, our, their.* The pronoun can be visible (stated) or invisible (implied). *Note: Its* (no apostrophe) is a possessive pronoun; *it's* (apostrophe) is a contraction meaning "it is." Begin absolute phrases with *its*, not *it's*.

Visible Pronoun: Mama was out of bed now, **her long black skirt over her night-gown.** *(The pronoun* her *is visible before "long black skirt," stated not implied.)*

John Steinbeck, "Flight"

Invisible Pronoun: He was sitting on his cot, **elbows on knees,** looking down. *(The word* his *is invisible before "elbows," implied not stated.)*

John Knowles, *A Separate Peace*

Note: See pages 173–79 for absolute phrases that function like adverbs.

Number: Sentences can contain either single or multiple absolute phrases:

Single—The men stepped out in evening clothes, and the women stepped out after them, **their hair coiffed up in elaborate detail.**

Ray Bradbury, *The Martian Chronicles*

Multiple—She stood by the window and watched her father water the flowers, **his head bent, his eyebrows raised.**

Jhumpa Lahiri, *Unaccustomed Earth*

Position: Absolute phrases occur in three positions:

Opener—**His hands raw,** he reached a flat place at the top.

Richard Connell, "The Most Dangerous Game"

S-V split—A wild-eyed horse, **its bridle torn and dangling,** trotted frantically through the mounds of men, tossing its head, whinnying in panic.

Lois Lowry, *The Giver*

Closer—The overalls of the workers were white, **their hands gloved with a pale corpse-colored rubber.**

Aldous Huxley, *Brave New World*

PRACTICE 1: MATCHING

Match the absolute phrase with the sentence. Write out each sentence, underlining the absolute phrase.

Sentences:

1. My mother and I saw each other frequently, ^.

   Barack Obama, *Dreams from My Father*

2. The men found Rosie the elephant lying on her side, quivering, ^.

   Sara Gruen, *Water for Elephants*

3. Some ants got out of the fire, ^, and went off not knowing where they were going.

   Ernest Hemingway, *A Farewell to Arms*

4. ^, he swayed where he stood and then fell flat on his face, stiff as a board.

   J. K. Rowling, *Harry Potter and the Sorcerer's Stone*

5. Slowly, ^, he lifted the truck in one powerful motion until the front was several inches off the ground and slowly walked it to the left of the road, where he set it down gently.

   Mildred D. Taylor, *Roll of Thunder, Hear My Cry*

Absolute Phrases:

a. their bodies burnt and flattened

b. his whole body rigid

c. our bond unbroken

d. his muscles flexing tightly against his thin shirt, sweat popping off his skin like oil on water

e. her foot still chained to a stake

PRACTICE 2: UNSCRAMBLING

Rearrange the scrambled list of sentence parts to match the structure of the model. Next, write an imitation of the model. Finally, identify the absolute phrases in the model and your imitation.

MODEL: A seared man, his charred clothes fuming where the blast had blown out the fire, rose from the curb.

   Fritz Leiber, "A Bad Day for Sales"

a. her jump rope hanging
b. scampered outside for recess
c. to her wrist
d. a little girl
e. where the teacher had attached it

PRACTICE 3: COMBINING

Combine the list of sentences into just one sentence that imitates the structure of the model. Next, write an imitation of the model. Finally, identify the absolute phrases in the model and your imitation.

MODEL: The wolf was almost as big as a calf, its coat as shaggy as a Russian hat, its fur black, its eyes a dark urine yellow.

Stephen King, *Just After Sunset*

a. The sun was low.
b. It was nearly as low as the garage roof.
c. Its rays were as penetrating as a needle's injection.
d. Its light was blinding.
e. Its heat was a raging unending inferno.

PRACTICE 4: IMITATING

Write an imitation of each model sentence so good that nobody can tell yours from the author's.

Models and Sample Imitations:

1. The superintendent, his head on his chest, was slowly poking the ground with his stick.

George Orwell, "A Hanging"

Sample: The intruder, his attention on the security system, was fearfully scanning the room for the switch.

2. [Their] eyes shining, [their] mouths open, triumphant, they savored the right of domination. *(Make your possessive pronouns invisible.)*

William Golding, *Lord of the Flies*

Sample: [Their] ears up, [their] tails wagging, hungry, the pups welcomed the vet with squeals.

3. She died in one of the downstairs rooms, in a heavy walnut bed with a curtain, her gray head propped on a pillow yellow and moldy with age and lack of sunlight.

William Faulkner, "A Rose for Emily"

Sample: She rested in the room with a view of the garden, on a soft roomy sofa with a footstool, her bandaged arm held in a sling colorful and decorated with autographs and drawings by her children.

PRACTICE 5: EXCHANGING

To practice writing good absolute phrases, exchange one of yours for the author's. Try to make yours as good as—maybe even better than—the author's.

Example:

Author's: Miss Hearne, **her face burning**, hardly listened to these words.

Brian Moore, *The Lonely Passion of Judith Hearne*

Yours: Miss Hearne, **her anger rising at Cranston's rude remark**, hardly listened to these words.

1. [My] **shoulder up**, I reeled around to face Boo Radley and his bloody fangs.

Harper Lee, *To Kill a Mockingbird*

2. Then he sat down, rigidly, **his elbow on the arm of the sofa** and **his chin in his hand**.

F. Scott Fitzgerald, *The Great Gatsby*

3. Valentine's pale skin seemed translucent, **its fairness accentuated by the cascade of white-blond hair that tumbled about her shoulders**.

Katherine Neville, *The Eight*

PRACTICE 6: EXPANDING

Partner with the author by creating an absolute phrase at the caret (^).

1. I scanned the street but saw only two soldiers, **their ^**, guarding the truck.

Roya Hakakian, *Journey from the Land of No*

2. For now, he could only sit on his suitcase, **his ^, his ^.**

> Markus Zusak, *The Book Thief*

3. In the long mirror across the room she saw herself, **her ^, her ^, her ^, her ^, her ^.**

> Dorothy Canfield Fisher, "The Apprentice"

COMPOSITION: Sports Report

ASSIGNMENT: Absolute phrases convey vivid, detailed description. Find a picture of an athlete in action in any sport—figure skating, hockey, basketball, boxing, football, baseball, diving, swimming, and so on. Pretend that you are a sports reporter hired to cover the event pictured.

Your job is to write up the event for readers of the sports news in a paper or electronic newspaper, <u>using varied absolute phrases</u>. In the following example, notice how absolute phrases convey action of the football player nicknamed "Darling" running down the field with the ball.

Example of a Sports Report (adapted)

The center floated by, **his hands desperately brushing Darling's knee as Darling picked his feet up high and delicately ran over a blocker and an opposing linesman in a jumble on the ground near the scrimmage line.** He smiled a little to himself as he ran, holding the ball lightly in front of him with his two hands, **his knees pumping high, his hips twisting in the almost girlish run of a back in a broken field.** The first halfback came at him, and he fed him his leg, then swung at the last moment, took the shock of the man's shoulder without breaking stride, ran through him, **his cleats biting securely into the turf.** There was only the safety man now, coming warily at him, **his arms crooked, hands spread.** Darling tucked the ball in, spurted at him, driving hard, hurling himself along, **his legs pounding, [his] knees high, [his] two hundred pounds bunched into controlled attack.** Without thought, **his arms and legs working beautifully together,** he headed right for the safety man, stiff-armed him, feeling blood spurt instantaneously from the man's nose onto his hand, seeing his face go awry, **[his] head turning, [his] mouth pulling to one side.**

> Irwin Shaw, "The Eighty-Yard Run"

Process:

- Picture the athlete in action.
- Narrate the beginning of the action in a way that attracts readers.

- Continue the narration by breaking down the action into separate components.

- Include an assortment of absolute phrases, each providing additional layers of description of the sports event you are reporting.

- Finish the paragraph with a memorable sentence.

"Nobody's a natural [athlete—or writer]. You work hard to get good and then work to get better. It's hard to stay on top."
—Paul Coffey, Hall of Fame athlete

Adjective Clause

In each pair, the second sentence has an adjective clause. Notice how it adds detail, elaboration, and style.

1a. My favorite teacher was Mr. Botte.

1b. My favorite teacher was Mr. Botte, **who taught biology and liked to animate the frogs and crawfish we had to dissect by making them dance in their waxed pans**. *(Adjective clause describes Mr. Botte.)*

> Alice Sebold, *The Lovely Bones*

2a. Louise tried to make talk, but the country boy was embarrassed and would say nothing.

2b. Louise, **whose mind was filled with thoughts of John Hardy**, tried to make talk, but the country boy was embarrassed and would say nothing. *(Adjective clause describes Louise.)*

> Sherwood Anderson, *Winesburg, Ohio*

3a. Beyond a fence, they came to the swimming pool.

3b. Beyond a fence, they came to the swimming pool, **which spilled over into a series of waterfalls and smaller rocky pools**. *(Adjective clause describes the swimming pool.)*

> Michael Crichton, *Jurassic Park*

4a. He could hear the first rumbles of thunder in the west.

4b. He could hear the first rumbles of thunder in the west, **where the clouds were stacking up**. *(Adjective clause describes the west.)*

> Stephen King, *Insomnia*

Adjective Group: The Describing Tools

WHAT IS AN ADJECTIVE CLAUSE? *It's a dependent clause describing a person, place, or thing.* Adjective clauses often begin with the words *who, whose, which, where.*

Number: Sentences can contain either single or multiple adjective clauses:

Single—The husband gazed wistfully at his wife, **whose face was becoming very pale.**

> Mark Twain, "The Man That Corrupted Hadleyburg"

Multiple—It was a living stone, **whose temperature was dependent on the hour, whose look of porousness would change depending on rain or a quick twilight.**

> Michael Ondaatje, *Anil's Ghost*

Position: Adjective clauses occur in two positions:

S-V split—Government aid, **which began with Lincoln,** took many forms.

> Stephen E. Ambrose, *Nothing Like It in the World*

Closer—At last she came to the end, to a wagon track, **where the silver grass blew between the red ruts.**

> Eudora Welty, "A Worn Path"

PRACTICE 1: MATCHING

Match the adjective clause with the sentence. Write out each sentence, underlining the adjective clause.

Sentences:

1. One figure, ^, tried to rise but could not.

   > Charles Frazier, *Cold Mountain*

2. In a few minutes they were joined by the shortstop Chuck Kellerman and Mr. Quint, ^.

   > Norman Katkov, "The Torn Invitation"

3. They were shown into the drawing room, ^.

   > Alexander Dumas, *The Count of Monte Cristo*

Adjective Clauses:

a. where the count had appeared five minutes earlier

b. whose wounds were so dreadful that he more resembled meat than man

c. which allows us to write whatever we please without fear of punishment

4. The good news is that we Americans are governed under a unique Constitution, ^.

   Kurt Vonnegut, "How to Write with Style"

   d. whose outlines remind us how detailed, vibrant, and alive are the things of this earth that perish

5. Sometimes one finds in fossil stones the imprint of a leaf, long since disintegrated, ^.

   Diane Ackerman, *A Natural History of the Senses*

   e. who taught chemistry and was assistant baseball coach

PRACTICE 2: UNSCRAMBLING

Rearrange the scrambled list of sentence parts to match the structure of the model. Next, write an imitation of the model. Finally, identify the adjective clauses in the model and your imitation.

MODEL: He balanced the tree branch in his hand for a moment, and then threw it with blinding speed, shattering it against another huge tree, which shook and trembled at the blow.

   Stephenie Meyer, *Twilight*

   a. passing it to a teammate
   b. who dodged
   c. and then kicked it with confident accuracy
   d. she maneuvered the soccer ball at her foot for five feet
   e. then moved toward the goal

PRACTICE 3: COMBINING

Combine the list of sentences into just one sentence that imitates the structure of the model. Next, write an imitation of the model. Finally, identify the adjective clauses in the model and your imitation.

MODEL: I rode upstairs in the elevator, stepped out, and went down the hall to Catherine's room, where I had left my white gown.

   Ernest Hemingway, *A Farewell to Arms*

   a. I stepped outside into the sunshine.
   b. I wandered about.
   c. And I looked over the garden to the back corner.
   d. The back corner was where we had planted many daylilies.

PRACTICE 4: IMITATING

Write an imitation of each model sentence so good that nobody can tell yours from the author's.

Models and Sample Imitations:

1. My brother Buckley went on a day-trip to the Museum of Natural History in New York, where he fell in love with the huge skeletons on display.

   Alice Sebold, *The Lovely Bones*

   Sample: My teacher arranged a field trip to the visitors center at Ellis Island near Manhattan, where we looked in awe at the amazing pictures of immigrants.

2. He led the sheep out to a piece of waste ground at the other end of the farm, which was overgrown with birch saplings.

   George Orwell, *Animal Farm*

   Sample: Alphonse put the assorted soups up on the top shelf in a corner of their pantry, which was filled with canned goods.

3. His mother, whose annuity wasn't quite enough in these days of inflation and high taxes, needed money.

   Saul Bellow, "A Father-to-Be"

   Sample: His teacher, whose understanding wasn't broad enough in this school of geniuses and high achievers, needed supervision.

PRACTICE 5: EXCHANGING

To practice writing good adjective clauses, exchange one of yours for the author's. Try to make yours as good as—maybe even better than—the author's.

Example:

Author's: He was quite tanned, and his hair, **which was almost exactly like his mother's in color and quality**, was a little sun-bleached on top.

   J. D. Salinger, "The Laughing Man"

Yours: He was quite tanned, and his hair, **which was tousled and messed up from the wind**, was a little sun-bleached on top.

1. I checked into the Paradise Hotel, **which proudly advertised hot and cold running water.**

   Michael Crichton, *Travels*

2. Suddenly, Alfred, **who heard the fight from across the street,** attacked from the rear with his favorite weapon, an indoor ball bat.

   John Steinbeck, *Cannery Row*

3. The orchards, **whose black branch tips had been inspected throughout the winter for latent signs of life,** suddenly bloomed, all at once.

   Barbara Kingsolver, *Animal Dreams*

PRACTICE 6: EXPANDING

Partner with the author by creating an adjective clause at the caret (^).

1. This boy was now a savage, whose ^.

   William Golding, *Lord of the Flies*

2. I keep seeing your face, which ^.

   James Baldwin, "Letter to My Nephew"

3. She lived in a small frame house with her invalid mother and a thin, sallow, unflagging aunt, where ^.

   William Faulkner, "Dry September"

COMPOSITION: Jigsaw Puzzle Paper

ASSIGNMENT: Are you ready for a challenge, a jigsaw puzzle with adjective clauses as the pieces? Below is a list of adjective clauses taken from sentences by authors. Write a paper that includes some of the adjective clauses in a way that makes sense for the piece you're writing. Build a sentence around that adjective clause as in the example below.

In your paper, <u>use at least five adjective clauses from the list below, as well as some of your own</u>. Since adjective clauses are sentence parts and not sentences, be sure to include all your adjective clauses within sentences.

Adjective Group: The Describing Tools

Example:

Adjective clause—whose illness had been diagnosed when she was eighteen

Nancy Mairs, *Plaintext*

*Sample sentence—*Away from home, where she had been virtually shut in for thirty years, cared for by hired nurses when her condition worsened beyond the ability of her parents to care for her, Janine, *whose illness had been diagnosed when she was eighteen,* an eternal optimist, adjusted quickly to the new routine in her new digs, a small assisted-living unit in a teaching hospital in Philadelphia.

People:

who for twenty years had been the town mystery

Sherwood Anderson, *Winesburg, Ohio*

who was big, handsome, and wild

Tracy Kidder, *Home Town*

who had brought flowers and baskets of fruit

Katherine Anne Porter, *Ship of Fools*

who taught chemistry and was assistant baseball coach

Norman Katkov, "The Torn Invitation"

whose disguise, eccentric air and gruesome appearance were causing a sensation

Gaston Leroux, *The Phantom of the Opera*

whose main interest in life was accumulating wealth

Judith Ortiz Cofer, *Silent Dancing*

Places:

where each morning between ten and eleven she would appear on the porch in a lace-trimmed boudoir cap

William Faulkner, "Dry September"

where a fire truck stood waiting

Keith Donohue, *The Stolen Child*

where he had been for ten days

Elliot Merrick, "Without Words"

where he set it down as gently as a sleeping child

Mildred D. Taylor, *Roll of Thunder, Hear My Cry*

where his uneasy steps halted

Harper Lee, *To Kill a Mockingbird*

where the only sign of his roommate was a khaki duffel bag and a canvas butterfly chair printed to resemble a gigantic hand

Anne Tyler, *Saint Maybe*

Things:

which had been combed wet earlier in the day

J. D. Salinger, "The Laughing Man"

which I also used to wipe the sweat from my face

Richard E. Kim, *Lost Names*

which he scratched continually

Robert Heinlein, *The Green Hills of Earth*

which made his jailer recoil in horror

Alexandre Dumas, *The Count of Monte Cristo*

which I began singing with only a bass accompaniment

Maya Angelou, *The Heart of a Woman*

which were printed on alternating sheets of the bathroom tissue

Ray Russell, "The Room"

which could not conceal the finely chiseled bones in their pitiable fleshlessness

Mary Elizabeth Vroman, "See How They Run"

SPECIAL FEATURE: Give your paper a creative title. What's a creative title? It's one that readers won't understand until after they finish the paper. In other words, the title doesn't predict what's in the paper. Only after reading the paper will readers understand why you used that title. Before selecting it, think of titles of movies or novels that fit the category of "creative" because they don't make sense until the end of the movie or the novel.

Examples:

Movies: *Slum Dog Millionaire, One Flew Over the Cuckoo's Nest, The Silence of the Lambs, Dr. Strangelove, The Dark Knight, Apocalypse Now, The Matrix*

Novels: *Gone with the Wind, To Kill a Mockingbird, Twilight, Lonesome Dove, The Bonfire of the Vanities, Invisible Man, The Catcher in the Rye, A Clockwork Orange*

Process:

- Before drafting your paper, study the adjective clauses for ideas for the content and form of your paper—an essay, a story, a poem, a song lyric, and so on.

- Choose one adjective clause at a time, and build a sentence around it, and then add more sentences linked in meaning.

- Aim for unusual ideas and content to captivate your reader's interest throughout the paper.

- End the paper with something that will linger in your reader's mind.

"A jigsaw puzzle has many pieces, and they all have to come together to make it work."
—Nido Qubein, author and motivational speaker

Reviewing the Adjective Tools

This section reviews all the sentence-composing tools from the adjective group. Once again you'll study the sentences of famous writer Stephen King. After a series of odd jobs as a janitor and an attendant at a Laundromat, Stephen King, writing during his time off, eventually earned a degree in 1970 and became an English teacher. One of the pieces he wrote, a draft of the novel *Carrie,* he threw into the garbage can. Fortunately his wife, Tabitha, retrieved it, and, after some reworking of the novel to his liking, King landed a publisher. *Carrie* was a popular novel, and later a popular movie. From both, he made enough money to work full-time as a writer. Over the years, Stephen King became one of the best-selling novelists ever, whose books have sold millions of copies.

In this review, analyzing sentences from Stephen King's works, you'll identify the adjective tools, and then imitate several of his sentences. Study how Stephen King skillfully builds his sentences, using the adjective tools you've learned.

"Good writing is about making good choices when it comes to picking the tools you plan to work with."
—Stephen King, *On Writing*

Directions: Using these abbreviations, identify the underlined tools. If you need to review the tool, study the pages below.

ADJECTIVE TOOLS	Review These Pages
opening adjective = OADJ	Pages 93–99
delayed adjective = DADJ	Pages 93–99
participial phrase = P	Pages 101–108
prepositional phrase = PREP	Pages 109–14
infinitive phrase = INF	Pages 115–20
absolute phrase = AB	Pages 121–27
adjective clause = DCADJ	Pages 129–36

Adjective Group: The Describing Tools

REVIEW 1: IDENTIFYING THE ADJECTIVE TOOLS

1. <u>Awake in his bed</u>, listening to one lonely dog bark in the distance, Wesley began to shiver.

   —UR

2. Stuart Redman, <u>who was perhaps the quietest man in town</u>, was sitting in one of the cracked plastic Woolco chairs, a can of beer in his hand, looking out the big service station window.

   —The Stand

3. Under the current, I saw decomposing bodies slipping by, <u>pulled by some deep current</u>.

   —Bag of Bones

4. Outside, <u>crossing the dark like a dream</u>, came the single bong of the clock in the town square.

   —Hearts in Atlantis

5. <u>With sudden dawning horror</u>, Bobby realized something was wrong with the pupils of Ted's eyes.

   —Hearts in Atlantis

6. If the contestant, <u>dizzy</u>, <u>breathless</u>, heart doing fantastic rubber acrobatics in his chest, missed the question, fifty dollars was deducted from his winnings, and the treadmill was speeded up.

   —The Running Man

7. I was in my 20's, <u>teaching high school English</u> and <u>working at an industrial laundry during the summer</u>, <u>washing motel sheets</u> and <u>occasionally driving a delivery truck around to those same motels</u>.

   —Just After Sunset

8. What happened was that hunters were afflicted by an anxiety <u>to make the shot</u>, <u>to get it over with one way or another</u>.

   —Dreamcatcher

9. The wolf was almost as big as a calf, <u>its coat as shaggy as a Russian hat</u>, <u>its fur black</u>, <u>its eyes a dark urine yellow</u>.

   —Just After Sunset

10. The months between March and June were a time <u>of conferences with doctors, of evening runs to the hospital with his wife, of trips to other hospitals in other states for special tests, of personal research in the Derry Public Library</u>, at first looking for answers the specialists might have overlooked, later on just looking for hope and grasping at straws.

> —*Insomnia*

REVIEW 2: IMITATING

For each model sentence, write the letter of its imitation. Then write your own imitation of the same model.

Group 1: Model Sentences

1. Awake in his bed, listening to one lonely dog bark in the distance, Wesley began to shiver.

2. Stuart Redman, who was perhaps the quietest man in town, was sitting in one of the cracked plastic Woolco chairs, a can of beer in his hand, looking out the big service station window.

3. Under the current, I saw decomposing bodies slipping by, pulled by some deep current.

4. Outside, crossing the dark like a dream, came the single bong of the clock in the town square.

5. With sudden dawning horror, Bobby realized something was wrong with the pupils of Ted's eyes.

Group 1: Imitations

a. Over the rainbow, I counted golden sparks rising up, lifted by some enchanting magic.

b. With unexpected deep joy, Sue Ellen felt everyone was applauding with the warmth of her acceptance.

c. Close to the ledge, looking down at the pin-sized people, the welder started to wave.

d. Overhead, flying the sky like a bird, was the silver body of the plane in the darkening sky.

e. Ellie Luvinski, who was probably the kindest girl on the team, was sobbing lots of those heartfelt, gentle tears, a water bottle in her hand, huddled over her injured teammate.

Group 2: Model Sentences

6. If the contestant, dizzy, breathless, heart doing fantastic rubber acrobatics in his chest, missed the question, fifty dollars was deducted from his winnings, and the treadmill was speeded up.

7. I was in my 20's, teaching high school English and working at an industrial laundry during the summer, washing motel sheets and occasionally driving a delivery truck around to those same motels.

8. What happened was that hunters were afflicted by an anxiety to make the shot, to get it over with one way or another.

9. The wolf was almost as big as a calf, its coat as shaggy as a Russian hat, its fur black, its eyes a dark urine yellow.

10. The months between March and June were a time of conferences with doctors, of evening runs to the hospital with his wife, of trips to other hospitals in other states for special tests, of personal research in the Derry Public Library, at first looking for answers the specialists might have overlooked, later on just looking for hope and grasping at straws.

Group 2: Imitations

f. The days of June, July, and August were months of blissful summer, of trips to the beach for sun and video games, of bone-chilling coconut snow cones eaten in the sweltering heat, of summer camps in sports at local schools, at first learning the rudiments of soccer, then just playing the sport and hanging out with other teenagers.

g. When the dancer, tentative, unsure, body gyrating to impossible choreography in the premiere, dropped a step, audience members were stunned in disbelief, and the curtain was rushed down.

h. He was in his teens, plodding through his suburban high school, and fantasizing about a breakthrough career as a rock star, writing hit songs, and energetically performing them before throngs of adoring women.

i. Her scream was nearly as overwhelming as her nightmare, its plot as grisly as a grotesque thriller, its horror indelible, its memory a deep surreal terror.

j. What happened was that the semifinalists were driven by a desire to raise the bar, to break every record that had ever been set.

Previewing the Adverb Tools

Adverbs <u>explain</u>. This section introduces you to the adverb group of sentence-composing tools: words, phrases, and clauses that *explain how, when, where,* or *why* something happened.

After this introduction, you'll focus on the particular explaining tools in the adverb group, learn about each tool in depth, practice using the tool through varied activities, and apply the tool in a piece of your writing.

These adverb tools explain **<u>how</u>** the salesman dropped the vase.

ADVERB WORDS	ADVERB PHRASES	ADVERB CLAUSES
Carelessly, the salesman dropped the vase.	The salesman dropped the vase, **one hand reaching to catch it.**	**As he fumbled with the wrapping**, the salesman dropped the vase.

These adverb tools explain **<u>when</u>** the car hit the curb.

ADVERB WORDS	ADVERB PHRASES	ADVERB CLAUSES
Suddenly, the car hit the curb.	The car, **in a flash**, hit the curb.	**Before the driver could react**, the car hit the curb.

These adverb tools explain **<u>where</u>** the flowers were destroyed.

ADVERB WORDS	ADVERB PHRASES	ADVERB CLAUSES
Everywhere, the flowers were destroyed.	**Throughout the garden**, the flowers were destroyed.	**Where the rain pelted them**, the flowers were destroyed.

These adverb tools explain **<u>why</u>** the instructor raised her voice.

ADVERB WORDS	ADVERB PHRASES	ADVERB CLAUSES
Purposely, the instructor raised her voice.	**To increase attention**, the instructor raised her voice.	The instructor raised her voice **because the excitement in the poem required more volume.**

ADVERB WORDS: Most adverbs end in *ly*.

Example:

<u>Gingerly</u>, he tried to slide his feet into the open maws of the stiff shoes, but they wouldn't go.

Louise Erdrich, *The Master Butchers Singing Club*

ADVERB PHRASES: There are three kinds of adverb phrases: prepositional, infinitive, absolute. All of them explain *how, when, where,* or *why* something happened.

1. **Prepositional Phrase**—Begins with a preposition: ***near*** *the store,* ***above*** *the sofa,* ***by*** *the computer,* ***in*** *the garden,* and so on.

Examples:

<u>With practice and concentration</u>, I was now able to decipher their speech. *(Explains <u>how</u> he deciphered their speech.)*

Keith Donohue, *The Stolen Child*

I read about it in the paper, <u>on my way to work</u>. *(Explains <u>when</u> the person read the paper.)*

James Baldwin, "Sonny's Blues"

A sharp current of pain ran <u>up his arm</u>, exploding in his shoulder. *(Explains <u>where</u> the pain was.)*

Robert Lipsyte, *The Contender*

<u>For food, a night's lodging, and the use of our piano</u>, he tuned it and gave Caroline and me free lessons. *(Explains <u>why</u> he tuned the piano and gave free lessons.)*

Katherine Paterson, *Jacob Have I Loved*

2. **Infinitive Phrase**—Begins with the word *to* plus a verb: <u>*to study*</u> *bugs,* <u>*to get*</u> *a new haircut,* <u>*to take*</u> *a computer apart.* These phrases always explain *why* something happened.

Examples:

<u>To avoid embarrassment</u>, all students quickly learned certain interviewing tricks. *(Explains why students learned the tricks.)*

Michael Crichton, *Travels*

Beulah, <u>to prove her absolute power in the classroom</u>, ignored the teacher. *(Explains why Beulah ignored the teacher.)*

Rosa Guy, *The Friends*

Webster combined the musical charm of his deep organ-like voice, a vivid imagination, an ability to crush his opponents with a barrage of facts, a confident and deliberate manner of speaking and a striking appearance, <u>to make his orations a magnet that drew crowds</u>. *(Explains why Webster's speeches drew a large audience.)*

John F. Kennedy, *Profiles in Courage*

---

3. **Absolute Phrase**—Those that function like adverbs explain <u>how</u> something happened. An absolute phrase is *almost* a complete sentence. You can make every absolute phrase a sentence by adding *was* or *were*.

Examples:

A teenager in a black tank top, <u>a greenish tattoo flowing across her broad back</u>, hoisted a toddler onto her shoulder.

Test: A greenish tattoo [was] flowing across her broad back. *(The absolute phrase explains how the teenager looked.)*

Barbara Kingsolver, *Animal Dreams*

A moment later, <u>both muffled so that they could hardly be seen in the dark corridors</u>, master and pupil left the room.

Test: Both [*were*] muffled so that they could hardly be seen in the dark corridors. *(The absolute phrase explains how they left the room.)*

C. S. Lewis, *The Chronicles of Narnia*

ADVERB CLAUSES: Most adverb clauses begin with *after, although, because, before, if, since, when, while*. They are sentence parts (<u>not</u> complete sentences) containing a subject (underlined <u>once</u>) and a verb (underlined <u>twice</u>).

after <u>the rain</u> <u>ended</u>	*although* <u>our team</u> <u>lost the game</u>
because <u>my computer</u> <u>crashed</u>	*before* <u>the test</u> <u>began</u>
if <u>the meeting</u> <u>is canceled</u>	*since* <u>folks</u> <u>live near a stream</u>
when <u>ants</u> <u>ruined the picnic</u>	*while* <u>the TV</u> <u>was broken</u>

Examples:

A turtle's heart will beat for hours *after* _he has been cut up and butchered_.

Ernest Hemingway, *The Old Man and the Sea*

Although _the villagers_ _had forgotten the ritual_ and _lost the original black box_, they still remembered to use stones.

Shirley Jackson, "The Lottery"

As _the trucks_ _pulled away_, the late afternoon sun came through the gray clouds for a moment.

Gerda Weissmann Klein, "All but My Life"

I wrote my first novel *because* _I_ _wanted to read it_.

Toni Morrison, novelist

Raisl, *before* _they_ _were married_, had made the bag out of a piece of her dress and embroidered it with the tablets of the Ten Commandments.

Bernard Malamud, *The Fixer*

If _we were late in reporting back to the airfield_, we had to do extra work.

Richard E. Kim, *Lost Names*

Since _we had little money_, we stopped near an artist who did portraits for two bucks apiece.

Pat Conroy, *My Losing Season*

When _he was nearly thirteen_, my brother Jem got his arm badly broken at the elbow.

Harper Lee, *To Kill a Mockingbird*

Ruthie was twisting her skirt in her hands, *while* _Winfield_ _dug a hole in the ground with his toe_.

John Steinbeck, *The Grapes of Wrath*

Review

Directions: For sentences with **boldfaced** *adverb tools*, exchange one of your own for the author's. For sentences with <u>deleted</u> *adverb tools*, expand the sentence by adding one of your own at the caret (^).

EXAMPLE OF EXCHANGING

Author's: To find a quieter location for the filming, Mrs. Cochran took me on a tour of the building.

Roya Hakakian, *Journey from the Land of No*

Yours: **To show off all of the improvements from the renovation**, Mrs. Cochran took me on a tour of the building.

EXAMPLE OF EXPANDING

Author's Sentence with Deleted Tool: **When ^**, Govinda rose.

Your Added Tool: **When he finished the final plan for the design of the apartment floor plan**, Govinda rose.

Original Sentence: **When the usual time of the exercise in meditation had passed**, Govinda rose.

Herman Hesse, *Siddhartha*

Adverb Words: Exchange the first five. Expand the next five.

1. As I watched him, he seemed to adjust himself a little, **visibly**.

   F. Scott Fitzgerald, *The Great Gatsby*

2. Speechless, Bryson scanned the small living room, **frantically**.

   Robert Ludlum, *The Prometheus Deception*

3. He brought his hands forward, **hard**.

   Stephen King, *Needful Things*

4. After ten minutes or so we got back in the car and drove out to the main road, **slowly** and **carefully**.

   Stephen King, *Everything's Eventual*

5. **Quickly** and **noisily**, Gerard came in.

> Elizabeth Bowen, "Foothold"

6. ^, two monstrous arms issued from the bosom of the waters and seized me by the neck, dragging me down to the depths with irresistible force.

> Gaston Leroux, *The Phantom of the Opera*

7. She had known it, ^, from the moment she read Graff's letter.

> Orson Scott Card, *Ender in Exile*

8. Someone was humming under her breath, ^.

> Ray Bradbury, *The Martian Chronicles*

9. ^ but ^, he walked toward her and the waiting chair.

> William P. Young, *The Shack*

10. He swam, ^, ^, his head always above the water.

> Jhumpa Lahiri, *Unaccustomed Earth*

Adverb Phrases: Exchange the first five. Expand the next five.

1. **To celebrate the opening of his new home**, Colonel Pyncheon gave a large party.

> Nathaniel Hawthorne, *House of the Seven Gables*

2. I made my way haltingly past the members of the choir with their black robes flapping in the morning breeze, **the doctor's words reverberating around me.**

> John Knowles, *A Separate Peace*

3. The elephant was dying, **in great agony**, very slowly.

> George Orwell, "Shooting an Elephant"

4. Some of the ten thousand stayed there **to clean, to haul,** and **to build things.**

> Toni Morrison, *Beloved*

5. The fight raged **down the steps** and **into the street** and **into the lot.**

> John Steinbeck, *Cannery Row*

6. In ^, Siddhartha spoke to Govinda.

   Hermann Hesse, *Siddhartha*

7. She poured the mess into a skillet, the eggs ^.

   Keith Donohue, *The Stolen Child*

8. On a late February morning, Indian Ed climbed across ^.

   Aron Ralston, *Between a Rock and a Hard Place*

9. We were sitting in the deep leather chairs, the champagne ^ and our glasses ^.

   Ernest Hemingway, *A Farewell to Arms*

10. Crocker insisted on staying on the east bank for ten days, to let ^ and to wait ^.

    Stephen E. Ambrose, *Nothing Like It in the World*

Adverb Clauses: Exchange the first five. Expand the next five.

1. **Before the store opened,** he sat on a step of the loading platform, observing a black beetle struggling on its back on the concrete of the parking lot.

   John Updike, *Terrorist*

2. The old woman and her daughter were sitting on their porch **when Mr. Shiftlet came up their road for the first time.**

   Flannery O'Connor, "The Life You Save May Be Your Own"

3. **If you know whence you came,** there is really no limit to where you can go.

   James Baldwin, "Letter to My Nephew"

4. Bombs in Central Europe were completely unreal to us here, not **because we couldn't imagine it** but **because our place here was too fair for us to accept something like that.**

   John Knowles, *A Separate Peace*

5. **If you could shut your ears to the sound of the sea, if you could forget how unvisited were the ferny coverts,** then there was a chance that you might put the beast out of mind and dream for a while.

   William Golding, *Lord of the Flies*

6. Swiftly, they climbed twenty feet up the largest tree, feeling for the branches, as the ^.

   Michael Crichton, *Jurassic Park*

7. He stared at the red, shivering reflection of a fire on the white wall of his tent until ^.

   Stephen Crane, *The Red Badge of Courage*

8. If ^, we would reduce our country's oil consumption by over 1.1 million barrels of oil every week.

   Barbara Kingsolver, *Animal, Vegetable, Miracle*

9. They came to Mars because ^, because ^, because ^.

   Ray Bradbury, *The Martian Chronicles*

10. It was dark when ^, frosty when ^.

    Julia Alvarez, "Snow"

---

*"Complications make eventually for simplicity,
and therefore I have always liked adverbial clauses."*
—Gertrude Stein, avant-garde writer

In the next pages, you'll learn and practice how authors use each of the tools in the adverb group to build their sentences, and how you can use them, too.

Opening and Delayed Adverbs

In each pair, the second sentence has an adverb in the opener or closer position. Notice how its position adds emphasis to the description.

1a. He liked the sound of the words.

1b. **Clearly**, he liked the sound of the words. *(The opening adverb emphasizes his liking the sound of the words.)*

Tracy Kidder, Mountains Beyond Mountains

2a. We touched the sheets covering the corpse at the edge of the fabric.

2b. We touched the sheets covering the corpse at the edge of the fabric, **gingerly**. *(The closer adverb shows their reluctance to touch the sheets.)*

Michael Crichton, Travels

WHAT IS AN OPENING ADVERB? *It's an adverb in the opener position of a sentence. It always <u>precedes</u> what is described.*

Number: Sentences can contain either single or multiple opening adverbs:

Single—**Certainly**, no one had ever played a piece of music for her before.

Ann Patchett, Bel Canto

Multiple—**Softly** but **persistently**, she was sobbing.

Keith Donohue, The Stolen Child

WHAT IS A DELAYED ADVERB? *It's an adverb placed after and away from the action described.*

Number: Sentences can contain either single or multiple delayed adverbs:

Single—What has changed, **decisively**, is the context in which the book might now be read.

Barack Obama, Dreams from My Father

Multiple—When he saw that I was looking at him, he closed his eyes, **sleepily**, **angelically**, then stuck out his tongue.

J. D. Salinger, "For Esme—with Love and Squalor"

Punctuation: For emphasis, a comma spotlights the adverb.

No comma—We touched the sheets covering the corpse at the edge of the fabric **gingerly**.

Comma—We touched the sheets covering the corpse at the edge of the fabric, **gingerly**. *(Here, the writer, using a comma for the adverb, emphasizes the manner of touching the sheets of the corpse.)*

The authors of the sentences selected for this section emphasize the manner of an action, so commas are used.

PRACTICE 1: MATCHING

Match the adverb with the sentence. Write out each sentence, underlining the opening or delayed adverb. *Note:* Many adverbs end in *ly*, but this practice contains some that don't.

Sentences:

1. ^, the road went down between the high green-colored banks.

   Eudora Welty, "A Worn Path"

2. The wind blew the red velvet rose petals all about, ^, and into small mounds of snow.

   Toni Morrison, *Song of Solomon*

3. After a while some of the younger boys came out on the bridge and began to jump off, ^, with whoops of fear.

   Marilynne Robinson, *Housekeeping*

4. ^, the sky was a fading strip of blue.
   Stephen King, *Bag of Bones*

5. Most of the acrid smoke from a yak dung fire under the teapot, ^, escaped through a large open square in the ceiling.

   Greg Mortenson and David Oliver Relin,
   Three Cups of Tea

Opening or Delayed Adverbs:

a. mercifully

b. up, down

c. overhead

d. cautiously and then exuberantly

e. deep, deep

PRACTICE 2: UNSCRAMBLING

Rearrange the scrambled list of sentence parts to match the structure of the model. Next, write an imitation of the model. Finally, identify the *opening adverbs* in the model and your imitation.

MODEL: Traditionally, employment and family dictate choices about where to live.

Barbara Kingsolver, *Animal, Vegetable, Miracle*

a. about where to vacation
b. determine decisions
c. and expenses
d. obviously
e. distance

PRACTICE 3: COMBINING

Combine the list of sentences into just one sentence that imitates the structure of the model. Next, write an imitation of the model. Finally, identify the *delayed adverbs* in the model and your imitation.

MODEL: For a moment he read to himself, but then his lips began to move, and in a moment he read aloud, slowly, pausing at the end of each line.

John Steinbeck, *Cannery Row*

a. This happened in the past.
b. What happened was that she sang for everyone.
c. But then her voice started to disintegrate.
d. And in the end she sang rarely, tentatively.
e. She was trembling at the beginning of each song.

PRACTICE 4: IMITATING

Write an imitation of each model sentence so good that nobody can tell yours from the author's.

Models and Sample Imitations:

1. Steadily, the room shrank, until the book thief could touch the shelves within a few small steps.

Markus Zusak, *The Book Thief*

Sample: Slowly, the moon rose, while the nocturnal animals would hunt their prey across the manicured back yard.

2. As I watched him, he seemed to adjust himself a little, visibly.

F. Scott Fitzgerald, *The Great Gatsby*

Sample: When I studied her, she began to preen herself a lot, flirtatiously.

3. He was clambering, heavily, among the creepers and broken trunks when a bird, a vision of red and yellow, flashed upwards with a witch-like cry.

William Golding, *Lord of the Flies*

Sample: She was sleeping, peacefully, among the sheets and soft covers when a noise, a sound of menace and danger, came quickly with a thunderlike snap.

PRACTICE 5: EXCHANGING

To practice writing good opening or delayed adverbs, exchange one of yours for the author's. Try to make yours as good as—maybe even better than—the author's.

Example:

Author's: He swam, **noisily**, **clumsily**, his head always above the water.

Jhumpa Lahiri, *Unaccustomed Earth*

Yours: He swam, **confidently**, **skillfully**, his head always above the water.

1. **Hesitantly** but **obediently**, he walked toward her and the waiting chair.

William P. Young, *The Shack*

2. Hacki moved toward the designated tree, **lightly**, **gracefully**, with an athlete's swift sureness.

Perri Knize, *A Piano Odyssey*

3. Andy Dufresne took the stand and told his story, **calmly**, **cooly**, and **dispassionately**.

Stephen King, "Rita Hayworth and Shawshank Redemption"

PRACTICE 6: EXPANDING

Partner with the author by creating an adverb at the caret (^).

1. In hunting season, all kinds of small game turn up in dumpsters, some of it, ^, not entirely dead.

   Lars Eighner, "On Dumpster Diving"

2. ^, ^, she curved herself around the box containing the new-born and wedged it into the backseat, where the pink blankets fell softly against the white vinyl upholstery.

   Kim Edwards, *The Memory Keeper's Daughter*

3. He stretched out his hands, ^, ^, waving them in the air to ward off the attack from the dinosaur he knew was coming.

   Michael Crichton, *Jurassic Park*

COMPOSITION: Performance Review

ASSSIGNMENT: Opening and delayed adverbs have descriptive power because their unusual placement spotlights them.

Find a picture of a performer in entertainment or sports—a rock star at a concert, a dancer in solo performance, an actor in a scene; a football player running for a touchdown, a basketball player jumping toward the hoop, a diver executing a championship dive, or some other performer or athlete. Pretend you are a journalist hired to cover that event for the entertainment or sports section of a print or electronic publication: newspaper, magazine, or website.

Somewhere within your coverage of the event, *include ten adverbs from the list below*. Build a sentence around each adverb, using it as an opening or delayed adverb. Occasionally use multiple adverbs, consecutive or nonconsecutive, within the same sentence. Aim for approximately 250 words to complete your coverage of the event.

absurdly	always	awkwardly	classically
accidentally	amazingly	badly	comically
admirably	ambitiously	beautifully	consecutively
adorably	artfully	blatantly	crudely
airily	artistically	boozily	cunningly

153

Adverb Group: The Explaining Tools

daftly
daintily
deliberately
delicately
delightfully
demurely
disgustedly
disgustingly
divertingly
drunkenly
dutifully
dynamically
eagerly
earnestly
ear-splittingly
ecstatically
eerily
effortlessly
elegantly
entrancingly
eternally
ethereally
euphorically
exactly
excellently
exceptionally
excitedly
extraordinarily
extravagantly

exuberantly
faithfully
famously
fancily
fantastically
fearlessly
fetchingly
flauntingly
foolishly
frozenly
fully
gaspingly
gaudily
gently
gigantically
goofily
gorgeously
gracefully
gradually
hair-raisingly
hastily
horizontally
horribly
huffily
hugely
humorously
hurriedly
hysterically
impressively

increasingly
infectiously
insolently
ironically
irrepressibly
jokingly
joltingly
joyously
jubilantly
kookily
light-footedly
lingeringly
loudly
lyrically
majestically
mesmerizingly
monotonously
noisily
noticeably
obviously
oddly
outrageously
overzealously
painstakingly
percussively
perfectly
perkily
playfully
powerfully

proudly
quaveringly
quickly
rakishly
rapturously
remarkably
repeatedly
rhythmically
ridiculously
rowdily
rudely
sacredly
satirically
saucily
self-confidently
slowly
smoothly
softly
soundly
spookily
spryly
startlingly
statuesquely
suddenly
superbly
sure-footedly
surprisingly
sweetly
tonelessly

tunefully	valiantly	weakly	wordlessly
tunelessly	violently	wearily	wretchedly
unavoidably	visibly	whimsically	yawningly
uncomfortably	vivaciously	wholeheartedly	yearningly
unexpectedly	vividly	wickedly	zanily
ungainly	vocally	wildly	zealously
ungracefully	voluptuously	woefully	zestfully
vainly	vulgarly	wonderfully	

Process:

- Early in the review, identify the setting, event, performer.

- Announce your response to the performance by telling your readers how good (or bad) the performance was.

- Support your opinion with examples from the performance.

- Arrange your review with some logical pattern: worst to best aspects, best to worst aspects, poor to poorest aspects, good to best aspects, or some other arrangement for reviewing a performance.

- Summarize your review with a sentence that recommends, or does not recommend, the performance for readers.

"The difference between the right word and the almost right word is the difference between lightning and the lightning bug."
—Mark Twain, author

Prepositional Phrase

In each pair, the second sentence has a prepositional phrase. Notice how it adds helpful information.

1a. Meg continued.

1b. Meg, **with the dogged determination that had so often caused her trouble,** continued. *(Explains how she continued.)*

> Madeleine L'Engle, *A Wrinkle in Time*

2a. He slept until almost eleven in the morning.

2b. **For the first time since his own undergraduate days**, he slept until almost eleven in the morning. *(Explains when he slept late.)*

> Stephen King, *UR*

3a. I was now able to decipher their language.

3b. **With practice and concentration over the years**, I was now able to decipher their language. *(Explains how the language became understandable.)*

> Keith Donohue, *The Stolen Child*

WHAT IS AN ADVERBIAL PREPOSITIONAL PHRASE? *A preposition is any word that will fit in this blank:* **It was _____ the box.** *about the box, at the box, beyond the box, from the box, near the box, over the box, under the box, inside the box, outside the box, by the box, and so on. Some prepositional phrases function like adverbs by answering one of these questions:*

Where? **Down the hall**, the others gathered like near relations at a funeral. *(Tells where they gathered.)*

> Sara Gruen, *Water for Elephants*

How? The tyrannosaur sank its jaws into the spare tire mounted on the back of the Land Cruiser, and, **in a single head shake**, tore it away. *(Tells how the tyrannosaur tore the tire off the Land Cruiser.)*

> Michael Crichton, *Jurassic Park*

Why? They'd moved from Brooklyn in the spring, **for Adam's job**. *(Tells why they moved.)*

> Jhumpa Lahiri, *Unaccustomed Earth*

When? **On a late February morning**, Indian Ed climbed across the rocks below the overhang where the team had spent the night with their cache of stolen goods—two pack animals, and a half dozen head of horses. *(Tells when this event happened.)*

Aron Ralston, Between a Rock and a Hard Place

Note: See pages 109–14 for prepositional phrases that function like adjectives.

Number: Sentences can contain either single, connected, or multiple prepositional phrases:

Single—**In her saner moments**, Alice could describe everything about the Sunday the mule kicked her in the head and sent all common sense flying out of her.

Edward P. Jones, The Known World

Connected—The whole congregation prayed for me alone, **in a mighty wail of moans and voices**. *(two connected prepositional phrases)*

Langston Hughes, The Big Sea

Multiple—We looked **around the house, under the table, in the closet's dark corners, in the toolbox, in the trash cans**. *(five nonconnected prepositional phrases)*

Jeannette Walls, The Glass Castle

Position: Prepositional phrases occur in three positions:

Opener—**With long brooms and steaming pails of water**, they washed the walls and the ceiling of the horse's stall.

Marguerite Henry, Misty of Chincoteague

S-V split—The country house, **on this particular wintry afternoon**, was most enjoyable.

James Thurber, "Mr. Monroe Holds the Fort"

Closer—The kitchen was the room Ruma was most proud of, **with its sandstone counters and cherry cupboards**.

Jhumpa Lahiri, Unaccustomed Earth

Adverb Group: The Explaining Tools

PRACTICE 1: MATCHING

Match the prepositional phrase with the sentence. Write out each sentence, underlining the prepositional phrase.

Sentences:

1. ^, there was no way to move products of any size from the territories in the West to markets on the East Coast or in Europe.

   Stephen E. Ambrose, *Nothing Like It in the World*

2. Jonas, ^, searched the auditorium for a glimpse of his father.

   Lois Lowry, *The Giver*

3. ^, there are words cut in the marble, which we are required to repeat to ourselves whenever we are tempted.

   Ayn Rand, *Anthem*

4. A few minutes later, ^ , the tall black man dribbled slowly from one end of the court to the other, and heaved the ball up into the air, and it dropped into the basket.

   Anne Lamott, *Bird by Bird*

5. ^, the wall collapsed.

   Brian W. Aldiss, "Who Can Replace a Man?"

Prepositional Phrases:

a. over the portals of the Palace of the World Council

b. amid a shower of dust

c. with still no score on the board

d. without railroads or rivers

e. from his place in the balcony

PRACTICE 2: UNSCRAMBLING

Rearrange the scrambled list of sentence parts to match the structure of the model. Next, write an imitation of the model. Finally, identify prepositional phrases in the model and your imitation.

MODEL: Bullets rained in the trees like the rattle of castanets, and the train, with a wounded creak, slowed to a halt.

Truman Capote, "A Ride Through Spain"

a. like the breath of winter
b. in the yards
c. snowflakes fell
d. with a contented sigh
e. and the houses
f. calmed
g. to a silence

PRACTICE 3: COMBINING

Combine the list of sentences into just one sentence that imitates the structure of the model. Next, write an imitation of the model. Finally, identify the prepositional phrases in the model and your imitation.

MODEL: Without any ritual, without ceremony, they savored the warm bread and shared the wine and laughed about the stranger moments of the weekend.

William P. Young, *The Shack*

a. We watched in silence.
b. We watched in awe.
c. What we watched were the baby animals.
d. And we enjoyed the sunshine and looked over the abundant fields of the farm.

PRACTICE 4: IMITATING

Write an imitation of each model sentence so good that nobody can tell yours from the author's.

Models and Sample Imitations:

1. Pennsylvania, with enormous deposits of both coal and iron, had more rail manufacturers than all of England.

Stephen E. Ambrose, *Nothing Like It in the World*

Sample: Elvira, under great pressure from both Mother and Father, had less noticeable concern than any of the others.

2. In that very first moment, when Houghton swished off the cloth, all Harrison had was a hunch, an instinctive sense that something was amiss.

Malcolm Gladwell, *Blink*

Sample: After a barely noticeable hesitation, when Henry stepped toward the window, all Shirley saw was a glimpse, a quick flash that revealed almost nothing.

3. Bobby saw, for just an instant, an incredibly tall, incredibly scrawny being standing inside a long yellow coat, a thing with flesh as white as new snow and lips as red as fresh blood.

   Stephen King, *Hearts in Atlantis*

Sample: Henry heard, with instant fear, a horribly long, horribly shrill scream coming from the second floor hallway, a yell with suddenness as quick as a lightning flash and terror as palpable as childhood nightmares.

PRACTICE 5: EXCHANGING

To practice writing good prepositional phrases, exchange one of yours for the author's. Try to make yours as good as—maybe even better than—the author's.

Example:

Author's: **In the darkness in the hallway by the door,** the sick woman arose and started again toward her own room.

   Sherwood Anderson, *Winesburg, Ohio*

Yours: **From her chair in the waiting room on her hospital floor,** the sick woman arose and started again toward her own room.

1. Mom, **in an unnaturally calm voice,** explained what had happened and asked if we could please have a ride to the hospital.

   Jeannette Walls, *The Glass Castle*

2. **In the hut in the patio,** the Indian waited the whole night long.

   Isabel Allende, *Daughter of Fortune*

3. **In the livid light of the fluorescent tube over the kitchen sink,** he made out a slender young man of about his own age, slumped like a question mark against the door frame.

   Michael Chabon, *The Amazing Adventures of Kavalier & Clay*

PRACTICE 6: EXPANDING

Partner with the author by creating a prepositional phrase at the caret (^).

1. **With** ^, he felt the tension drain away, replaced by a deep sense of relief.

   William P. Young, *The Shack*

2. **In** ^, where a dance was to be held, the fiddlers tuned their instruments.

   Sherwood Anderson, "Sophistication"

3. Janet and the Tiger went racing back, **over** ^ and **over** ^, **over** ^, **across** ^ and **along** ^.

   Joan Aiken, *A Necklace of Raindrops*

COMPOSITION: Presidential Paragraph

ASSIGNMENT: Write a presidential sentence similar in style to the sentences below of President Lincoln or President Obama. Use three prepositional phrases, each beginning with the same word, to make your sentence memorable. Then, build a presidential paragraph around that sentence.

In his second inaugural speech, President Abraham Lincoln, trying to heal the hurt of a nation reeling from its civil war, said these memorable words, introduced by three prepositional phrases of the same length all beginning with the same preposition: *with.*

> *(1) **With** malice toward none, (2) **with** charity for all, (3) **with** firmness in the right, as God gives us to see the right, let us strive on to finish the work we are in, to bind up the nation's wounds.*

President Barack Obama, emphasizing aspects of a struggle for justice in America, also used three prepositional phrases, but of different lengths:

> *We are struggling (1) **between** worlds of plenty and worlds of want, (2) **between** the modern and the ancient, (3) **between** those who embrace our teeming, colliding, irksome diversity, while still insisting on a set of values that binds us together, and those who would seek, under whatever flag or slogan or sacred text, a certainty and simplification that justifies cruelty toward those not like us.*

   Barack Obama, *Dreams from My Father*

Process:

- Analyze why Lincoln and Obama arranged their three prepositional phrases as they did.

- Decide the most effective arrangement of your three prepositional phrases.

- After writing your presidential sentence, add to it by writing a presidential paragraph suitable for a public address by a president of a business, an organization, or a country.

"At a political rally, a woman yelled to the presidential candidate,
'You, sir, have the vote of every thinking person.' The candidate replied,
'That's not enough, madam. To win, we need a majority.' "
—Adlai L. Stevenson, during his run for United States president in 1956

Infinitive Phrase

In each pair, the second sentence has an adverb infinitive. Notice how it adds detail, elaboration, and style.

1a. I decided that I would watch the elephant for a while, and then go home.

1b. I decided that I would watch the elephant for a while **to make sure that the animal did not turn savage again**, and then go home. *(Adverb infinitive explains why he watched the elephant.)*

George Orwell, "Shooting an Elephant"

2a. We tried to think of word games.

2b. **To keep ourselves from going crazy from boredom**, we tried to think of word games. *(Adverb infinitive explains why they tried to think of word games.)*

Barbara Kingsolver, *The Bean Trees*

3a. When Ulysses S. Grant and Robert E. Lee met in the parlor of a modest house at Appomattox Court House, Virginia, on April 9, 1865, a great chapter in American life came to a close, and a great new chapter began.

3b. When Ulysses S. Grant and Robert E. Lee met in the parlor of a modest house at Appomattox Court House, Virginia, on April 9, 1865, **to work out the terms for the surrender of Lee's Army of Northern Virginia**, a great chapter in American life came to a close, and a great new chapter began. *(Adverb infinitive explains why Grant and Lee met.)*

Bruce Catton, *The American Story*

WHAT IS AN ADVERB INFINITIVE PHRASE? *It's a phrase that <u>explains</u> why something happened and that always begins with* to *plus a verb: to sing, to read, to linger, to laugh, to sigh, to study, and so on.*

Infinitive phrases can explain something (like adverbs), or name something (like nouns), or describe something (like adjectives).

1. *Adverb infinitive*—The team from Western High School worked overtime **to make it to the final round of the playoffs**. *(The infinitive <u>explains why</u> the team worked overtime. Adverb infinitives answer the question "Why?")*

2. *Noun infinitive*—**To make it to the final round of the playoffs** was the team's goal. *(The infinitive <u>names</u> the team's goal. Noun infinitives answer the question "What?" See pages 43–47.)*

3. *Adjective infinitive*—The coach emphasized the need **to make it to the final round of the playoffs.** *(The infinitive <u>describes</u> the need. Adjective infinitives answer the question "What kind?" See pages 115–20.)*

Number: Sentences can contain either single or multiple adverb infinitives:

Single—I've heard there are monks who sit with dead bodies, who sit in bone yards, cemeteries, or crypts **to make friends with eternity.** *(Explains why those monks sit with dead bodies.)*

David Guterson, *The Other*

Multiple—The nurses stayed **to wipe the saliva that drooled from his mouth, to irrigate the big craters of bedsores that covered his hips, to suction the lung fluids that threatened to drown him, to clean the feces that burned his skin like lye, to pour the liquid food down the tube attached to his stomach, to put pillows between his knees to ease the bone-on-bone pain, to turn him every hour to keep the bedsores from getting worse,** and **to change his gown and linen every two hours to keep him from being soaked in perspiration.** *(Explains why the nurses stayed to care for this patient.)*

Barbara Huttmann, "A Crime of Compassion"

PRACTICE 1: MATCHING

Match the adverb infinitive with the sentence. Write out each sentence, underlining the adverb infinitive.

Sentences:

1. Carefully taking the burning match from his friend's fingertips, he set it in the bowl, and in short order we started a fire ^.

    Keith Donohue, *The Stolen Child*

2. ^, it is instructive to listen to the imperatives most frequently issued to professional football players by their coaches, teammates, and fans.

    John McMurtry, "Kill 'Em! Crush 'Em! Eat 'Em Raw!"

Adverb Infinitives:

a. to qualify for the racing team in junior high

b. to catch the larger problems of subject and form

3. My mother told me about dressing in her best party clothes on Saturday nights and going to the town's plaza ^.

    c. to toast our palms and fingertips

    Judith Ortiz Coffer, "The Myth of the Latin Woman"

4. Most writers scan their draft, reading as quickly as possible ^, then move in closer and closer as they read and write, reread and rewrite.

    d. to grasp some of the more conspicuous similarities between football and war

    Donald M. Murray, "The Maker's Eye: Revising Your Own Manuscripts"

5. ^, she would have to practice every day.

    e. to promenade with her girlfriends in front of the boys they liked

    Eleanor Coerr, *Sadako and the Thousand Paper Cranes*

PRACTICE 2: UNSCRAMBLING

Rearrange the scrambled list of sentence parts to match the structure of the model. Next, write an imitation of the model. Finally, identify the infinitives in the model and your imitation.

MODEL: To avoid embarrassment and to make the job easier, all students quickly learned certain interviewing tricks.

    Michael Crichton, *Travels*

    a. very successful employees
    b. to guarantee success
    c. most applicants quietly observed
    d. and to complete the test successfully

PRACTICE 3: COMBINING

Combine the list of sentences into just one sentence that imitates the structure of the model. Next, write an imitation of the model. Finally, identify the adverbial infinitives in the model and your imitation.

MODEL: The tenant men squatted down on their hams again to mark the dust with a stick, to figure, to wonder.

    John Steinbeck, *The Grapes of Wrath*

a. The excited children gathered.
b. The gathering was around their teacher now.
c. They gathered to hear the results of the contest.
d. They gathered to cheer.
e. They gathered to celebrate.

PRACTICE 4: IMITATING

Write an imitation of each model sentence so good that nobody can tell yours from the author's.

Models and Sample Imitations:

1. Shoulder up, I reeled around to face Boo Radley and his bloody fangs.

> Harper Lee, *To Kill a Mockingbird*

Sample: Anger over, I sat down to contemplate my punishment and its complete inequity.

2. They dropped his belongings at the freshman dorm, where the only sign of his roommate was a khaki duffel bag and a canvas butterfly chair printed to resemble a gigantic hand.

> Anne Tyler, *Saint Maybe*

Sample: We took the uniforms to the music room, where the only evidence of the band was an opened trumpet case and an empty hat rack designed to hold the band's hats.

3. Raoul, his throat filled with sobs, oaths and insults, fumbled awkwardly at the great mirror that had opened to let Christine pass to the murky Phantom's dwelling below.

> Gaston Leroux, *The Phantom of the Opera*

Sample: Linda, her curiosity heightened by rumors, stories and dares, strode tentatively toward the trap door that had lifted to lead others down to the subterranean giant's den underneath.

PRACTICE 5: EXCHANGING

To practice writing good adverb infinitives, exchange one of yours for the author's. Try to make yours as good as—maybe even better than—the author's.

Example:

Author's: **To keep away the evil omen of thirteen from their homes,** families spent the day outdoors.

Roya Hakakian, *Journey from the Land of No*

Yours: **To escape the heat and humidity inside their homes during the 19th century,** families spent the day outdoors.

1. Later, I stumbled around **to find more branches to throw on the flames.**

   David Guterson, *The Other*

2. As I had often done for dying soldiers, I sang **to pass the time** and **to distract him from his pain.**

   Amelia Atwater-Rhodes, *Hawksong*

3. When the children went on a hike, she packed bird and flower guides into their knapsacks, and quizzed them on their return **to see if they had learned anything**.

   Wallace Stegner, *Crossing to Safety*

PRACTICE 6: EXPANDING

Partner with the author by creating an infinitive phrase at the caret (^).

1. **To ^**, she was forced to sell her last valuable possession, her husband's sewing machine.

   John Hersey, *Hiroshima*

2. Seventeenth century European women and men sometimes wore beauty patches in the shape of hearts, suns, moons, and stars, applying them to their breasts and faces **to ^**.

   Diane Ackerman, "The Face of Beauty"

3. **To ^** , Mrs. Cochran took me on a tour of the building.

   Roya Hakakian, *Journey from the Land of No*

COMPOSITION: A Great Start

The beginning of a piece of writing—story, report, essay, research paper, or any piece of writing—is crucial to captivating your reader. A reader gives a writer time and concentration to receive some benefit from reading the writer's piece. Beginning a piece of writing well starts that reciprocity of benefit between reader and writer.

ASSIGNMENT: Pretend you are one of the authors below who has written the first sentence of a long story. Choose one of their sentences as the first sentence in a paragraph that will begin that story:

1. Then the hungry men crowded the alleys behind the stores to beg for bread, to beg for rotting vegetables, to steal when they could.

   John Steinbeck, *The Grapes of Wrath*

2. The suitcase was tied with a belt to keep it from popping open.

   Lorenz Graham, "Hitchhiker"

3. The Monster twitched its jeweler's hands down to fondle at the men, to twist them in half, to crush them like berries, to cram them into its teeth and its screaming throat.

   Ray Bradbury, "A Sound of Thunder"

4. There is a spider, in the bathroom, of uncertain lineage, bulbous at the abdomen and drab, whose six-inch mess of web works somehow, works miraculously, to keep her alive and me amazed.

   Annie Dillard, "Death of a Moth"

5. He turned to face his sleeping grandson, the long lashes and rounded cheeks reminding him of his own children when they were young.

   Jhumpa Lahiri, *Unaccustomed Earth*

Next, create the rest of the paragraph. Just as the authors' sentences use various sentence-composing tools, <u>including infinitive phrases</u>, use within your paragraph sentence-composing tools to make your paragraph memorable. *Reminder:* Don't try to write a complete story. Write, revise, and finalize only the first paragraph of that story—although you may want at another time to finish your story.

Process:

- Begin your paragraph with one of the authors' sentences above.

- Continue with a thread mentioned in the first sentence—a detail, a place, a person, an idea. Zoom in to focus the reader's attention.

- Conclude with a sentence that ends the paragraph without forecasting the rest of the story but compelling the reader to continue.

"I do a great deal of rewriting. With the beginning of a book, I will often rewrite the first paragraph, and the first few pages, thirty and forty times, because another belief I have is that in that moment, in those first crucial paragraphs and pages, all the reader's decisions are made."
—Brian Moore, novelist

Absolute Phrase

In each pair, the second sentence has an absolute phrase. Notice how it adds detail, elaboration, and style.

1a. In pregnancy she seemed to him beautiful but fragile.

1b. In pregnancy she seemed to him beautiful but fragile, **fine blue veins faintly visible through her pale white skin.** *(Absolute phrase tells how she seemed beautiful but fragile.)*

> Kim Edwards, *The Memory Keeper's Daughter*

2a. One clean-shaven man was sleeping.

2b. One clean-shaven man was sleeping, **papers strewn around him.** *(Absolute phrase tells how the man was sleeping.)*

> Jeffrey Sachs, *The End of Poverty*

3a. Dawn was starting to break over the mountain peaks.

3b. Dawn was starting to break over the mountain peaks, **the colors of early morning sunrise beginning to identify themselves against the ashy gray of the escaping night.** *(Absolute phrase tells how the dawn broke over the mountain peaks.)*

> William P. Young, *The Shack*

WHAT IS AN ABSOLUTE PHRASE? *It's a phrase telling how something happened.* An absolute phrase is <u>almost</u> a complete sentence. As a test, you can make every absolute phrase into a sentence by adding *was* or *were*.

Examples:

1. He sat facing the door and the windows, a book in his hand.

> Yann Martel, *Life of Pi*

  Test: A book [*was*] in his hand.

2. They walked in silence for a moment through the fragrant woods, **the rusty pine needles gentle under their feet.**

> Madeleine L'Engle, *A Wrinkle in Time*

Test: The rusty pine needles [*were*] gentle under their feet.

Absolutes that function as adverbs usually tell <u>how</u> something in the rest of the sentence occurred.

Note: See pages 121–27 for absolute phrases that function like adjectives.

Number: Sentences can contain either single or multiple absolute phrases:

Single—Two hard-faced men, **both cradling submachine guns**, stood watching him closely from the adjacent guard station.

> Robert Ludlum, *The Moscow Vector*

Multiple—They were walking in the direction of Robbie's apartment now, **the leaves rattling around their feet, a quarter moon flying through the wind-driven clouds overhead.**

> Stephen King, *UR*

Position: Absolute phrases occur in three positions:

Opener—**Pain shooting up my entire arm**, I lay panting on the edge of the pool and gingerly began to feel my wrist.

> Theodore Taylor, *The Cay*

S-V split—A teenager in a black tank top, **a greenish tattoo flowing across her broad back**, hoisted a toddler onto her shoulder.

> Barbara Kingsolver, *Animal Dreams*

Closer—The instructor, noting my activity, came back from an adjoining desk, **a smile on his lips**.

> James Thurber, "University Days"

PRACTICE 1: MATCHING

Match the absolute phrase with the sentence. Write out each sentence, underlining the absolute phrase.

Sentences:

1. Suddenly, he was exhausted, ^.
   William P. Young, *The Shack*

Absolute Phrases:

a. the two large dark eyes watching him coldly

2. It's beyond my skill as a writer to capture that day [9-11-2001], ^.

   Barack Obama, *Dreams from My Father*

b. the cold sinking night air shifting the heat of the day up

3. There is a hot breeze blowing through the window, ^.

   Alexandra Fuller, *Don't Let's Go to the Dogs Tonight*

c. the planes vanishing into steel and glass, the slow-motion cascade of the towers crumbling into themselves, the ash-covered figures wandering the streets

4. All about, like a moving current, a mountain river, came the new air, ^.

   Ray Bradbury, *The Martian Chronicles*

d. the oxygen blowing from the green trees

5. Amid the ferns, Grant saw the head of an animal, motionless, partially hidden in the fronds, ^.

   Michael Crichton, *Jurassic Park*

e. the myriad of emotions taking their toll

PRACTICE 2: UNSCRAMBLING

Rearrange the scrambled list of sentence parts to match the structure of the model. Next, write an imitation of the model. Finally, identify the absolute phrases in the model and your imitation.

MODEL: My first memory is of awakening in a makeshift bed, dried snot caked in my nose and mouth, under a blanket of reeds.

   Keith Donohue, *The Stolen Child*

   a. under a sky of blue
   b. on a velvet lawn
   c. her fondest dream was of napping
   d. bright sun shining on her face and body

PRACTICE 3: COMBINING

Combine the list of sentences into just one sentence that imitates the structure of the model. Next, write an imitation of the model. Finally, identify the absolute phrases in the model and your imitation.

MODEL: There was something about a saloon that always turned me into an awful liar, the lies streaming out of me at sixty miles an hour.

Robert Cormier, Take Me Where the Good Times Are

 a. There was the joke about a huge mouse.
 b. It was the joke that always turned me into a giggling fool.
 c. The giggles were obscuring the words of the joke.
 d. They obscured the words for my listeners.

PRACTICE 4: IMITATING

Write an imitation of each model sentence so good that nobody can tell yours from the author's.

Models and Sample Imitations:

1. A teenager in a black tank top, a greenish tattoo flowing across her broad back, hoisted a toddler onto her shoulder.

Barbara Kingsolver, Animal Dreams

Sample: Our teacher for the writing course, a pile of papers waiting for his careful attention, read our essays about technical processes.

2. We watched from the upper bleachers as riders pounded past us at full gallop, yipping and yelling, foam flying from their horses' mouths.

Khaled Hosseini, The Kite Runner

Sample: Barbara watched from the judging booth as skaters glided over the ice at high speeds, twirling and dancing, ice shavings shooting from their skate blades.

3. The raptor struck out with its hind claws, and with a single swift movement ripped open the belly of the fallen animal, coils of intestine falling out like fat snakes.

Michael Crichton, Jurassic Park

Sample: The gymnast reached up with his calloused hands, and in a balanced fluid arc rode around the center of the high bar, pieces of hand-chalk landing like powdery snow.

PRACTICE 5: EXCHANGING ————————————————————

To practice writing good absolute phrases, exchange one of yours for the author's. Try to make yours as good as—maybe even better than—the author's.

Example:

Author's: She watched the children troop in noisily, **ancient nursery rhymes running through her head.**

> Mary Elizabeth Vroman, "See How They Run"

Yours: She watched the children troop in noisily, **teachers trying to subdue their shouting and boisterous behavior.**

1. His voice was rich calypso, soft and musical, **the words rubbing off like velvet.**
   > Theodore Taylor, *The Cay*

2. Then, slowly, he fell to his knees and pitched forward onto the road, **the blood pooling red on the black asphalt.**
   > Robert Ludlum, *The Moscow Vector*

3. I hitched my boat to the pine and started at a trot for the back porch, **a bucket of hard crabs in one hand** and **a fistful of money in the other.**
   > Katherine Paterson, *Jacob Have I Loved*

PRACTICE 6: EXPANDING ————————————————————

Partner with the author by creating an absolute phrase at the caret (^).

1. He handed me a bound black notebook, the kind schoolchildren use for their lessons, **the ^**.
   > Keith Donohue, *The Stolen Child*

2. In the brown gloom of the cellar, her face was white, **the ^**.
   > Bill and Vera Cleaver, *Where the Lilies Bloom*

3. Laughing and shoving restlessly, damp-palmed with excitement, the spectators came shuffling into the great concrete stadium, **some ^, some ^, some ^**.
   > Steve Allen, "The Public Hating"

COMPOSITION: Creative Narrative

ASSIGNMENT: Multiple absolute phrases can convey events happening all at once. Here, for example, is a sentence by Ray Bradbury from *The Martian Chronicles* explaining through multiple absolute phrases the events of a quiet morning on the planet Mars:

> *It was quiet in the deep morning of Mars, stars shining in the canal waters, the children curled with their spiders [Martian pets] in closed hands, the lovers arm in arm, the moons gone, the torches cold, the stone amphitheaters deserted.*

Bradbury's sentence describes how six different events happened that morning on Mars. His sentence explaining those events combines a series of six short sentences converted to absolute phrases:

1. Stars [*were*] shining in the canal waters.

2. The children [*were*] curled with their spiders in closed hands.

3. The lovers [*were*] arm in arm.

4. The moons [*were*] gone.

5. The torches [*were*] cold.

6. The stone amphitheaters [*were*] deserted.

For a creative narrative, choose one of these sentences, or one of your own like them, and <u>add four or more absolute phrases</u>.

It was a noisy night in the dorm.

It was a hilarious moment at the party.

It was a happy time for the family.

It was a perfect vacation with friends.

It was a moment to linger in memory.

It was a thrilling event.

It was a history-making happening.

Follow that sentence with a narrative telling what happened next.

Process:

- Start with the sentence that names the event, followed by multiple absolute phrases.

- Narrate other events that followed, using more absolute phrases and other sentence-composing tools.

- End the piece with a summary of what happened.

"People call me a science fiction writer, but I don't think that's quite true. I think that I'm a magician who is capable of making things appear and disappear right in front of you, and you don't know how it happened."
—Ray Bradbury, author (and word magician)

Adverb Clause

In each pair, the second sentence has an adverb clause. Notice how it adds detail, elaboration, and style.

1a. We spent hours discussing our childhood pets, how much we missed them and how we longed someday to own a dog again.

1b. **When we were dating, long before children ever came on our radar**, we spent hours discussing our childhood pets, how much we missed them and how we longed someday to own a dog again. *(Adverb clause explains when they discussed pets.)*

> John Grogan, *Marley & Me*

2a. It is one of the town's two apartment houses, the second being a ramshackle mansion known as the Teacherage.

2b. It is one of the town's two apartment houses, the second being a ramshackle mansion known, **because a good part of the local school's faculty lives there**, as the Teacherage. *(Adverb clause explains why the mansion is called the "Teacherage.")*

> Truman Capote, *In Cold Blood*

3a. Snow billowed, stinging her face.

3b. Snow billowed, stinging her face, **when she opened the car door.** *(Adverb clause explains when the snow stung her face.)*

> Kim Edwards, *The Memory Keeper's Daughter*

WHAT IS AN ADVERB CLAUSE ? *It's a dependent clause that explains something about the rest of the sentence.* Adverb clauses answer these questions, and begin with the words in parentheses (called *subordinating conjunctions*):

When did it happen? *(after, as, before, when, while, until)*

Why did it happen? *(because, since)*

How did it happen? *(as if, as though)*

Under what condition did it happen? *(although, if)*

Adverb Group: The Explaining Tools

Number: Sentences can contain either single or multiple adverb clauses:

Single—That night in our room, **although I was worn out from all the exercise,** I tried to catch up on what had been happening in trigonometry.

John Knowles, *A Separate Peace*

Multiple—He struck again and again, **until the buzzard lay dead, until its head was a red pulp.**

John Steinbeck, *The Red Pony*

Position: Adverb clauses occur in three positions:

Opener—**While the children stood half squabbling by the window,** their father leaned over a sofa in the adjoining room above a figure whose heart in sleep had quietly stopped its beating.

Algernon Blackwood, "The Tradition"

S-V split—Happiness, **if he had the right to use that word,** was something that until now he had only experienced in music.

Ann Patchett, *Bel Canto*

Closer—He was showing me the porcupine's tail and guiding my hand along by holding my wrist, **when he suddenly gave it a sharp push upward so that I squeaked with pain.**

Robert Russell, *To Catch an Angel*

Adverb Group: The Explaining Tools

PRACTICE 1: MATCHING

Match the adverb clause with the sentence. Write out each sentence, underlining the adverb clause.

Sentences:

1. Love touched the hearts of the Brahmans' young daughters ^.
   Hermann Hesse, *Siddhartha*

2. ^, I would have tried to talk her in off the ledge and maybe placate her with a goldfish.
   John Grogan, *Marley & Me*

3. President Roosevelt, ^, seemed a haggard old man.
   David McCullough, *Truman*

4. ^, you always see the signs of it in the sky for days ahead.
   Ernest Hemingway, *The Old Man and the Sea*

5. ^, in fact we inhabit the same state, the State of Fear.
   Michael Crichton, *State of Fear*

Adverb Clauses:

a. if there is a hurricane

b. when Siddhartha walked through the lanes of the town with the luminous forehead, with the eye of a king, with his slim hips

c. if Jenny really only wanted a dog to hone her parenting skills

d. although we imagine we live in different nations—France, Germany, Japan, the U. S.

e. although he was only two years older than Truman

PRACTICE 2: UNSCRAMBLING

Rearrange the scrambled list of sentence parts to match the structure of the model. Next, write an imitation of the model. Finally, identify the adverb clauses in the model and your imitation.

MODEL: Dad and some of his Air Force buddies were on a cliff of the canyon, trying to work up the nerve to dive into the lake forty feet below, when Mom and a friend drove up.
   Jeannette Walls, *The Glass Castle*

   a. were by the fountain in the plaza
   b. hoping to figure out a way to get away

183

c. when chaperones and a guard approached them

d. Donald and a few of his friends

e. from the museum right behind them

PRACTICE 3: COMBINING

Combine the list of sentences into just one sentence that imitates the structure of the model. Next, write an imitation of the model. Finally, identify the adverb clauses in the model and your imitation.

MODEL: When a gun goes off on a cold winter's day, the retort echoes through the forest for miles around, and every living creature stops to look and listen.

Keith Donohue, *The Stolen Child*

a. This happens when the sun rises up in a liquid gray sky.

b. The light stretches through the clouds in silver shafts.

c. And all waking persons want to rise.

d. And those persons want to begin.

PRACTICE 4: IMITATING

Write an imitation of each model sentence so good that nobody can tell yours from the author's.

Models and Sample Imitations:

1. The porch light, when I came up the hill from the stable, did not cheer me.

Wallace Stegner, *Crossing to Safety*

Sample: The falling darkness, as I looked out the window from my room, did not discourage me.

2. After Edgar stuffed a brat into a bun and scooped potato salad onto his plate, Henry gestured toward the white parcel on the table.

David Wroblewski, *The Story of Edgar Sawtelle*

Sample: While Beth stretched one sheet across the bed and pulled clean cases onto her pillows, Dotty crossed to the single chair in the room.

3. After everything was pinned down and neat and in its place, when everything was safe and certain, when the towns were well enough fixed and the loneliness was at a minimum, then the sophisticates came in from Earth.

Ray Bradbury, *The Martian Chronicles*

Sample: When papers were turned in and graded and out of sight, when classes were over and done, when the campus was almost empty and the students were on their vacations, then the faculty went out for lunch.

PRACTICE 5: EXCHANGING

To practice writing good adverb clauses, exchange one of yours for the author's. Try to make yours as good as—maybe even better than—the author's.

Example:

Author's: **When her sweetheart went away,** people hardly saw her at all.

> William Faulkner, "A Rose for Emily"

Yours: **When Janine became depressed,** people hardly saw her at all.

1. She ran, limping and sobbing, **until she reached the big wrought iron gate.**

   > Cornelia Funke, *Inkheart*

2. **Because I had a fairly large vocabulary and had been reading constantly since childhood,** I had taken words and the art of arranging them too lightly.

   > Maya Angelou, *The Heart of a Woman*

3. Inman had fired his rife **until his right arm was weary from working the ramrod, until his jaw was sore from biting the ends off the paper cartridges.**

   > Charles Frazier, *Cold Mountain*

PRACTICE 6: EXPANDING

Partner with the author by creating an adverb clause at the caret (^).

1. When ^, Hassan and I used to climb the poplar trees in the driveway of my father's house and annoy our neighbors by reflecting sunlight into their homes with a shard of mirror.

   > Khaled Hosseini, *The Kite Runner*

2. He shuddered gently, as though ^.

   > Kurt Vonnegut, *Breakfast of Champions*

3. Kids wanted to fight us because ^, because ^, because ^, because ^, because ^.

   > Jeannette Walls, *The Glass House*

COMPOSITION: Jigsaw Puzzle Paper

ASSIGNMENT: Here is a jigsaw puzzle with adverb clauses as the pieces. Below is a list of adverb clauses taken from sentences by authors. Write a paper that includes some of the adverb clauses in a way that makes sense for the piece you're writing. Build a sentence around that adverb clause as in the example below

    In your paper, <u>use at least five adverb clauses from the list below, as well as some of your own</u>. Since adverb clauses are sentence parts and not sentences, be sure to include all your adverb clauses within sentences.

Example:

Adverb clause—as streaks of light appeared in the east
> James A. Michener, *The Bridges at Toko-Ri*

Sample sentence—The darkness of the kitchen, <u>as streaks of light appeared in the east</u>, seemed almost pleasant, perhaps because Delbert loved to awaken for coffee before going to the field for the endless baling of hay, an annual monotony, relieved somewhat by the iPod in his ear blaring headbanger rock anthems.

When Did It Happen?

as she stepped into the light
> Ray Bradbury, *The Martian Chronicles*

as twilight began to fall
> Carl Stephenson, "Leiningen Versus the Ants"

as the handle of the gun hit the skin over the bone, and the small man was knocked to the ground
> Ann Patchett, *Bel Canto*

as the boat bounced from the top of each wave
> Stephen Crane, "The Open Boat"

before he reached his shack
> Ernest Hemingway, *The Old Man and the Sea*

before the bell rang
> Mary Elizabeth Vroman, "See How They Run"

when his shaking had subsided a little

> John Steinbeck, *Cannery Row*

when she looked at the children and saw how tired they were

> John Hersey, *Hiroshima*

when the gun crashed and the barrel-flash made a picture on his eyes

> John Steinbeck, *The Pearl*

Why Did It Happen?

because I pulled its whiskers

> Joan Aiken, *A Necklace of Raindrops*

because he was still able to move his hands

> Mitch Albom, *Tuesdays with Morrie*

because of the routines we follow

> Maya Angelou, *Wouldn't Take Nothing for My Journey Now*

because he's worried about his hair falling out

> Margaret Atwood, "Fiction: Happy Endings"

because my work was in a field that brought me into contact with the people who produced television shows

> Lynn Caine, *Lifelines*

because it wasn't an empty, shutting-out-people silence but a quiet, friendly thing

> Robert Cormier, *Take Me Where the Good Times Are*

because she was only fifteen and busy with her growing up

> Lloyd C. Douglas, *The Robe*

since he didn't come to help me

> Langston Hughes, *The Big Sea*

since we had little money

> Pat Conroy, *My Losing Season*

since he was a strong, good-looking boy

> Barbara Kingsolver, *Pigs in Heaven*

How Did It Happen?

as if he had cold slimy water next to his skin

> James Joyce, *Portrait of the Artist as a Young Man*

as if she were going to meet someone round the corner

> Virginia Woolf, *To the Lighthouse*

as if she were trying to draw all the breath out of him.

> Flannery O'Connor, "Good Country People"

as though thousands of nails had been scraped against a blackboard

> Gaston Leroux, *The Phantom of the Opera*

as though nothing had happened

> Harper Lee, *To Kill a Mockingbird*

Under What Condition Did It Happen?

although they lived in style

> D. H. Lawrence, "The Rocking-Horse Winner"

although good looks may rally one's attention

> Diane Ackerman, "The Face of Beauty"

although I now know that most adolescents feel out of step much of the time

> Judith Ortiz Cofer, "The Myth of the Latin Woman"

although he tried not to think of it

> Bernard Malamud, "The Prison"

although they must all have known that he was dead drunk, and seen the danger he would soon be in

Alan Sillitoe, *Saturday Night and Sunday Morning*

if he could be very honest

Ann Patchett, *Bel Canto*

if someone he liked explained things

John Steinbeck, *The Red Pony*

if the weather were mild enough

James Hilton, *Goodbye, Mr. Chips*

SPECIAL FEATURE: Give your paper a creative title. What's a creative title? It's one that readers won't understand until after they finish the paper. In other words, the title doesn't predict what's in the paper. Only after reading the paper will readers understand why you used that title. Before selecting it, think of titles of movies or novels that fit the category of "creative" because they don't make sense until the end of the movie or the novel:

Examples:

Movies: *Slum Dog Millionaire, One Flew Over the Cuckoo's Nest, The Silence of the Lambs, Dr. Strangelove, The Dark Knight, Apocalypse Now, The Matrix*

Novels: *Gone with the wind, To Kill a Mockingbird, Twilight, Lonesome Dove, The Bonfire of the Vanities, Invisible Man, The Catcher in the Rye, A Clockwork Orange*

Process:

- Before drafting your paper, study the adverb clauses for ideas for the content and form of your paper—an essay, a story, a poem, a song lyric, and so on.

- Choose one adverb clause at a time and build a sentence around it, and then additional sentences linked in meaning.

- Aim for unusual ideas and content to captivate your reader's interest throughout the paper.

- Include adverb clauses about people, places, things, some selected from the above list, others created by you.

- In your creative paper, in addition to adverb clauses use other sentence-composing tools to enhance your writing.

- End the paper with something that will linger in your reader's mind.

"A writer has to know how to manage a long sentence gracefully, how to make it as clear and as vigorous as a series of short ones."
—Joseph M. Williams, *Style: Ten Lessons in Clarity and Grace*

Reviewing the Adverb Tools

This section reviews all the sentence-composing tools from the adverb group, once again through the sentences of famous writer Stephen King.

A prolific writer, writing every day of his life except holidays, King has sold more than 100 million copies of his books, with five of them simultaneously on the *New York Times* best-seller list, setting a record for most titles at the same time. Also an avid reader, attributing his development as a writer to the influences of hundreds of authors whose works he read, King epitomizes the read-write connection, the link between focused reading and focused writing.

In this review, analyzing sentences from Stephen King's works, you'll identify the adverb tools, and then imitate several of his sentences. Study how Stephen King skillfully builds his sentences, using the adverb tools you've learned.

Directions: Using these abbreviations, identify the underlined tools. If you need to review the tool, study the pages below.

ADVERB TOOLS	Review These Pages
opening adverb = OADV	Pages 149–55
delayed adverb = DADV	Pages 149–55
prepositional = PREP	Pages 157–63
infinitive = INF	Pages 165–71
absolute = AB	Pages 173–79
adverb clause = ADVC	Pages 181–90

REVIEW 1: IDENTIFYING THE ADVERB TOOLS

1. Carol got slowly to her feet, using the trunk of the tree <u>to support her back</u>.
   —*Hearts in Atlantis*

2. <u>Faintly</u>, beyond the wall, came the sounds of the Overlook Hotel's kitchen, gearing down from lunch.
   —*The Shining*

3. Bobby saw, <u>for just an instant</u>, an incredibly tall, incredibly scrawny being standing inside a long yellow coat, a thing with flesh as white as new snow and lips as red as fresh blood.
   —*Hearts in Atlantis*

4. He sat up suddenly, <u>the smell of burnt matches fluffing out from his suit and making me feel all gaggy in my throat</u>.

> —*Everything's Eventual*

5. <u>As my hand closed around the candles</u>, the lights in the house went out, and the only electricity was the lightning in the sky.

> —*The Mist*

6. <u>Behind them</u>, <u>in the park</u>, a dog barked, and someone shouted.

> —*Cell: A Novel*

7. The Old Crocks gathered <u>to play chess</u>, <u>to play gin</u>, or just <u>to shoot the bull</u>.

> —*Insomnia*

8. After ten minutes or so we got back in the car and drove out to the main road, <u>slowly</u> and <u>carefully</u>.

> —*Everything's Eventual*

9. They were walking in the direction of Robbie's apartment now, <u>the leaves rattling around their feet</u>, <u>a quarter moon flying through the wind-driven clouds overhead</u>.

> —*UR*

10. She must have just climbed out of the water, <u>because she was still dripping</u> and <u>because her hair was plastered against her cheeks</u>.

> —*Bag of Bones*

REVIEW 2: IMITATING

For each model sentence, write the letter of its imitation. Then write your own imitation of the same model.

Group 1: Model Sentences

1. Carol got slowly to her feet, using the trunk of the tree to support her back.

2. Faintly, beyond the wall, came the sounds of the Overlook Hotel's kitchen, gearing down from lunch.

3. Bobby saw, for just an instant, an incredibly tall, incredibly scrawny being standing inside a long yellow coat, a thing with flesh as white as new snow and lips as red as fresh blood.

4. He sat up suddenly, the smell of burnt matches fluffing out from his suit and making me feel all gaggy in my throat.

5. As my hand closed around the candles, the lights in the house went out, and the only electricity was the lightning in the sky.

Group 1: Imitations

a. Eloise turned around coyly, a twinkle of capricious mischief darting out from her eyes and making me recall the pranks of our childhood.

b. When my heart broke after the fight, the hope for our romance died abruptly, and my only feeling was the despair of the dejected.

c. Harold sat tentatively on the step, taking this break from the party to consider his options.

d. Charlotte heard, for just a split second, a jarringly loud, jarringly shrill shout rising above a dark, dank pond, a note with volume as piercing as booming thunder and duration as quick as lightning flash.

e. Abruptly, inside the kitchen, rose the steam of the owner's whistling teapot, breaking up the quiet.

Group 2: Model Sentences

6. Behind them, in the park, a dog barked, and someone shouted.

7. The Old Crocks gathered to play chess, to play gin, or just to shoot the bull.

8. After ten minutes or so we got back in the car and drove out to the main road, slowly and carefully.

9. They were walking in the direction of Robbie's apartment now, the leaves rattling around their feet, a quarter moon flying through the wind-driven clouds overhead.

10. She must have just climbed out of the water, because she was still dripping and because her hair was plastered against her cheeks.

Group 2: Imitations

f. After a half an hour or so we walked down to the pier and strolled out to the jetty's end, lazily and happily.

g. He was rounding a curve on the joyride with his new motorcycle then, traffic flanking the cycle, the adjacent drivers watching with heightened vigilance for the cyclist nearby.

h. Near me, in the theatre, a cell phone rang, and the audience booed.

i. The smaller children congregated to play hopscotch, to play jacks, or just to play any game.

j. Donnell could not cross to the corner, because the light was then changing and because the traffic was speeding through the intersection.

"Try to remember that grammar is for the world as well as for school."
—Stephen King, *Everything's Eventual*

Multiple Tools

In each pair, the second sentence has multiple tools. Notice how the multiple tools add detail and style to the sentence.

1a. Siddhartha knew many venerable Brahmans, chiefly his father.

1b. Siddhartha knew many venerable Brahmans, chiefly his father, **the pure one, the scholar, the most venerable one.** *(Noun Tools: Multiple appositive phrases name the identities of Siddhartha's father.)*

   Hermann Hesse, *Siddhartha*

2a. He fractured his skull.

2b. He **fractured his skull**, **broke two ribs**, and **suffered a shattered hip**, which was replaced with some exotic combination of Teflon and metal. *(Verb Tools: Multiple verbs narrate three injuries.)*

   Stephen King, *Dreamcatcher*

3a. Don Allman was in the office.

3b. Don Allman was in the office, **wearing headphones, correcting papers, and singing about Jeremiah the bullfrog in a voice that went beyond the borders of merely bad and into the unexplored country of the execrable.** *(Adjective Tools: Multiple participial phrases describe his activities.)*

   Stephen King, *UR*

4a. Kids wanted to fight us.

4b. Kids wanted to fight us **because we had red hair, because Dad was a drunk, because we wore rags and didn't take as many baths as we should have, because we lived in a falling-down house partly painted yellow and had a pit filled with garbage in front, because they'd go by our dark house at night and see that we couldn't even afford electricity.** *(Adverb Tools: Multiple adverb clauses explain why kids wanted to fight.)*

   Jeannette Walls, *The Glass Castle*

WHAT ARE MULTIPLE TOOLS? *They are a series of two or more of the same tool within the same sentence.* They usually occur as openers, S-V splits, or closers.

   In the practices with multiple tools, you will be working with all of the sentence-composing tools in this worktext. To review any of them, study the page indicated.

Reviewing the Sentence-Composing Toolbox

NOUN GROUP: THE NAMING TOOLS

In New York, **the most important state in any Presidential race**, and **a state where politics were particularly sensitive to the views of various nationality and minority groups**, Democrats were joyous and Republicans angry and gloomy.

John F. Kennedy, Profiles in Courage

He kept **slipping into deep drifts of snow**, and **skidding on frozen puddles**, and **tripping over fallen tree trunks**, and **sliding down steep banks**, and **barking his shins against rocks until he was wet and cold and bruised all over**.

C. S. Lewis, The Chronicles of Narnia

At nine o'clock Earth started **to explode**, **to catch fire**, and **to burn**. *(The noun infinitives name what started.)*

Ray Bradbury, The Martian Chronicles

The first moment I saw you I knew **that you wanted a bicycle, that getting one was very important to you**, and **that you meant to earn the money for one this summer if you could**.

Stephen King, Hearts in Atlantis

PRACTICE 1: MATCHING AND IMITATING

Match the multiple noun tool with its sentence. Write out the sentence, and then imitate it. Name the noun tools in the model and your imitation: *appositive phrases, gerund phrases, infinitive phrases,* or *noun clauses*.

Sentences:

1. Beneath the dragon, under all his limbs and his huge coiled tail, and about him on all sides stretching away across the unseen floors, lay countless piles of precious things, ^.

   J. R. R. Tolkien, The Hobbit

Noun Tools:

a. that the last words he said to his father were very angry words and that there could never be any reconciliation between them in this life

2. He believed the only three valid purposes microwaves served were ^.

   Stephen King, *Needful Things*

3. What grieved my father bitterly was ^.

   Marilynne Robinson, *Gilead*

4. Grant squeezed his fists together, and bit his lip, trying desperately ^.

   Michael Crichton, *Jurassic Park*

5. The true nature of the damage to the Titanic may be partly revealed as exploration of the wreck continues over the coming years, but it will often be hard to tell ^.

   Walter Lord, *The Night Lives On*

b. re-heating coffee, making popcorn, and putting some heat on take-out from places like Cluck-Cluck Tonite

c. what was done by the iceberg and what was caused by the impact as the ship struck the ocean floor

d. gold wrought and unwrought, gems and jewels, and silver red-stained in the ruddy light

e. to remain motionless, to make no sound to alert the tyrannosaur

PRACTICE 2: EXPANDING

Partner with the author by creating multiple noun tools at the carets (^). Use the type indicated.

Appositive Phrases:

1. There was a speck above the island, ^, ^.

   William Golding, *Lord of the Flies*

2. When the girls were born, expensive gifts arrived, ^ and ^.

   Jhumpa Lahiri, *Unaccustomed Earth*

3. The park had the usual attractions, ^, ^, ^, ^, ^, and ^.

   Mitch Albom, *The Five People You Meet in Heaven*

Gerund Phrases:

4. ^, ^, and ^ are all part of the excitement.

   Charles R. Joy, "Hindu Girl of Surinam"

5. His parents had furnished the house by ^ and by ^.

> P. D. James, *A Certain Justice*

6. ^, ^, ^, and ^ are exhilarating.

> Mary Ann Shaffer and Annie Barrows, *The Guernsey Literary and Potato Peel Pie Society*

Infinitive Phrases:

7. He taught me to ^, to ^, to ^.

> Perri Knize, *A Piano Odyssey*

8. He found himself wanting to ^, to ^, to ^, to ^.

> Kim Edwards, *The Memory Keeper's Daughter*

Noun Clauses:

9. He thought about how ^, and how ^.

> John Steinbeck, *The Red Pony*

10. That ^ and that ^ barely registered in my mind.

> Barack Obama, *Dreams from My Father*

VERB GROUP: THE NARRATING TOOLS

MULTIPLE VERB .... page 67

Our father, dreaming bitterly of Barbados, despised and mocked by his neighbors and ignored by his sons, **held down his unspeakable factory job, spread his black gospel in bars on the weekend,** and **drank his rum.**

> James Baldwin, *Tell Me How Long the Train's Been Gone*

INVERTED VERB .... page 73

On the other end of the dining room **was a tall marble fireplace**, always lit by the orange glow of a fire in the wintertime, and **were pictures of ancestors**, hung randomly on the wall.

> Khaled Hosseini, *The Kite Runner*

PRACTICE 3: MATCHING AND IMITATING

Match the verb tool with its sentence. Write out the sentence. Using that sentence as a model, imitate it. Name the verb tools in the model and your imitation: *multiple verb* or *inverted verb.*

Sentences:

1. Her father lived alone now, ^.

   Jhumpa Lahiri, *Unaccustomed Earth*

2. On the trees hang almost no more harvest and ^.

   Sherwood Anderson, *Winesburg, Ohio*

3. Against the white marble mantelpiece stood Eugene and ^.

   Elizabeth Bowen, "Foothold"

4. After deciding he would get nothing of interest from the two old men who comprised the entire staff of "The Weekly Islander," the feature writer from the Boston "Globe" took a look at his watch, ^.

   Stephen King, "Colorado Kid"

5. Kino's hand leaped to catch the scorpion crawling down the rope that held the baby's hammock, but it fell past his fingers, ^.

   John Steinbeck, *The Pearl*

Verb Tools:

a. remarked that he could just make the one-thirty ferry back to the mainland if he hurried, thanked them for their time, dropped some money on the table cloth, weighted it down with the salt shaker so the onshore breeze wouldn't blow it away, and hurried down the stone steps

b. fell on the baby's shoulder, landed, and struck

c. are only a few gnarled apples that the pickers have rejected

d. leaned his wife

e. made his own meals

PRACTICE 4: EXPANDING

Partner with the author by creating multiple noun tools at the carets (^). Use the type indicated.

Multiple Verb:

1. At nine o'clock, one morning late in July, Gatsby's gorgeous car ^ and ^.

   F. Scott Fitzgerald, *The Great Gatsby*

2. One morning, when his son Rudolph had gone to town in the car, leaving a work team idle in his barn, his father ^, ^, and ^.

   Willa Cather, "Neighbor Rosicky"

3. Polly ^, ^, and ^, feeling meaner than a snapping turtle on account of not sleeping well.

   Bill Brittain, *The Wish Giver*

4. In a matter of seconds they ^, ^, ^, and then ^.

   Christy Brown, *My Left Foot*

5. The boat ^, ^, ^, ^, and ^.

   Stephen King, *It*

Inverted Verb:

6. In the room by the window overlooking the land that had come down to him was ^ and sat ^.

   Sherwood Anderson, *Winesburg, Ohio*

7. Only towards noon and in the early afternoon, when the sun sat high in the sky, was there ^ and occurred ^.

   Peter Abrahams, *Tell Freedom*

8. Above, about, within it all, was ^, and on every side of him towered ^.

   Willa Cather, "Paul's Case"

9. On a tarnished gilt easel before the fireplace stood ^ and appeared ^.

   William Faulkner, "A Rose for Emily"

10. In the kitchen of the flat in Green Point there were ^, and there stood ^.

    J. M. Coetzee, *Disgrace*

ADJECTIVE GROUP: THE DESCRIBING TOOLS

Rain-drenched, fresh, vital, full of life, spring enveloped all of us.

Mildred D. Taylor, *Roll of Thunder, Hear My Cry*

A voice suddenly shouted at me, **loud** and **strong** and **angry**, although I couldn't understand the words.

Robert Cormier, *Take Me Where the Good Times Are*

Swollen to the top of its banks, clouded dark brown with silt, belching dirt and stones, and **carrying blown branches along in its torrent**, it had turned into an ugly, angered river.

Bill and Vera Cleaver, *Where the Lilies Bloom*

They tiptoed from room to room, afraid to speak above a whisper and gazing with a kind of awe **at the unbelievable luxury, at the beds with their feather mattresses, the looking-glasses, the horsehair sofa, the Brussels carpet, the lithograph of Queen Victoria over the drawing-room mantelpiece.**

George Orwell, *Animal Farm*

It was the time **to accomplish his mission** or **to fail.**

Walter Dean Myers, *Legend of Tarik*

She burst into great sobs, **her whole body shaking, her tears streaming down her face.**

Michael Crichton, *Travels*

She failed to see a shadow, **which followed her like her own shadow, which stopped when she stopped**, and **which started again when she did.**

Gaston Leroux, *The Phantom of the Opera*

PRACTICE 5: MATCHING AND IMITATING

Match the multiple adjective tool with its sentence. Write out the sentence. Using that sentence as a model, imitate it. Name the adjective tools in the model and your imitation: *opening adjectives, delayed adjectives, participial phrases, prepositional phrases, infinitive phrases, absolute phrases,* or *adjective clauses.*

Sentences:

1. ^, Carlotta flung herself into her part in the opera without restraint of modesty.

   Gaston Leroux, *The Phantom of the Opera*

2. Our fist-fight, at recess, ended with my knees buckling and my lip bleeding while my friends, ^, watched resignedly.

   Jon Katz, "How Boys Become Men"

3. On that fishing trip, I took along my son, ^.

   E. B. White, "Once More to the Lake"

4. ^, we worked all morning in opposite parts of the woods.

   Truman Capote, *The Grass Harp*

5. A tall boy with glittering golden hair and a sulky mouth pushed and jostled a light wheel chair along, in which sat a small weary dying man, ^.

   Katherine Anne Porter, *Ship of Fools*

Adjective Tools:

a. calling to each other, hooting like owls loose in the daytime

b. his weak dark whiskers flecked with gray, his spread hands limp on the brown blanket over his knees, his eyes closed

c. certain of herself, certain of her friends in the audience, certain of her voice and her success

d. who had never had any fresh water up his nose and who had seen lily pads only from train windows

e. sympathetic but out of range

PRACTICE 6: EXPANDING

Partner with the author by creating multiple adjective tools at the carets (^). Use the type indicated.

Opening Adjectives:

1. ^ and ^, he really felt as if the whole car were moving beneath him.

    Michael Crichton, *Jurassic Park*

Delayed Adjectives:

2. He looked as if he were fourteen or fifteen, ^ and ^, in tennis shoes and blue jeans.

    Langston Hughes, "Thank You, M'am"

Participial Phrases (present):

3. They lived together in peace and happiness, ^, ^, and ^.

    Elizabeth Coatsworth, *The Story of Wang Li*

Participial Phrases (past):

4. Against the wall in the hall downstairs near the cloak-stand was a coffin-lid, ^, ^.

    Leo Tolstoy, "The Death of Ivan Ilyich"

Prepositional Phrases:

5. The nurses would try to get him into the bathtub on Saturday nights, calling his name down the hallways, but he'd hide someplace in ^ or under ^ or in ^.

    Robert Cormier, *Take Me Where the Good Times Are*

Infinitive Phrases:

6. I discovered a new way to ^ and a new way to ^.

    Christy Brown, *My Left Foot*

Absolute Phrases:

7. She forgot even her sorrow at the sharp report of his gun and the piteous sight of thrushes and sparrows dropping silent to the ground, their ^ and their ^.

    Sarah Orne Jewett, "A White Heron"

Adjective Clauses:

8. We knew that one room in the attic, which ^, and which ^.

   William Faulkner, "A Rose for Emily"

9. To Richardson, whose ^, and whose ^, this pause was a long horror.

   Stephen Crane, "Horses—One Dash"

10. The confused man, who ^ and who ^, thought for a moment.

   James Thurber, "The Unicorn in the Garden"

ADVERB GROUP: THE EXPLAINING TOOLS

Quickly and **quietly**, over the guard's head, George walked away.

   Hans Augusto Rey, *Curious George*

After a while some of the younger boys came out on the bridge and began to jump off, **cautiously** and then **exuberantly**, with whoops of fear.

   Marilynne Robinson, *Housekeeping*

To his home, to his comfort, to the bringing up of their children, to the garden and her greenhouse, to the local church, and **to her patchwork quilts,** Margaret had happily given her life.

   P. D. James, *A Certain Justice*

The nurses stayed **to wipe the saliva that drooled from his mouth, to irrigate the big craters of bedsores that covered his hips, to suction the lung fluids that threatened to drown him, to clean the feces that burned his skin like lye, to pour the liquid food down the tube attached to his stomach, to put pillows between his knees to ease the bone-on-bone pain, to turn him every hour to keep the bedsores from getting worse,** and **to change his gown and linen every two hours to keep him from being soaked in perspiration.**

   Barbara Huttmann, "A Crime of Compassion"

The newcomers so forlorn, and **the old dog team so worn out**, the outlook was anything but bright.

Jack London, *The Call of the Wild*

They waited until tonight **because nobody could see them at night, because Atticus would be so deep in a book he wouldn't hear the Kingdom coming, because if Boo Radley killed them they'd miss school instead of vacation, and because it was easier to see inside a dark house in the dark than in the daytime.**

Harper Lee, *To Kill a Mockingbird*

PRACTICE 7: MATCHING AND IMITATING———————————

Match the multiple adverb tool with its sentence. Write out the sentence. Using that sentence as a model, imitate it. Name the adverb tools in the model and your imitation: *opening adverbs, delayed adverbs, prepositional phrases, absolute phrases, adverb clauses.*

Sentences:

1. With a gentle forefinger, he stroked the turtle's throat and chest ^.

   John Steinbeck, *The Red Pony*

2. I heard them beyond the corral, ^.

   Joseph Krumgold, *And Now Miguel*

3. ^, there is no excuse for the kind of blind craving for power and resources that provoked the wars of previous generations.

   Martin Luther King, Jr., *Where Do We Go from Here: Community or Chaos?*

4. He swam, ^, his head always above the water.

   Jhumpa Lahiri, *Unaccustomed Earth*

Adverb Tools:

a. the dog barking and the lamb making its kind of noise and the ewe making her kind of noise

b. progressively and inexorably

c. in this day of man's highest technical achievement, in this day of dazzling discovery, of novel opportunies, loftier dignities and fuller freedoms for all

d. until the horny-toad relaxed, until its eyes closed, and until it lay languorous and asleep

5. ^, as I moved through high school,   e. noisily, clumsily
   college, and pro leagues, my body
   was dismantled, piece by piece, by
   football injuries.

>   John McMurtry, "Kill 'Em! Crush 'Em! Eat 'Em Raw!"

PRACTICE 8: EXPANDING

Partner with the author by creating multiple adverb tools at the carets (^). Use the type indicated.

Opening Adverbs:

1. ^, ^, I ploughed through the whole twenty-six letters of the alphabet with my mother and gradually mastered each of them in turn.

>   Christy Brown, *My Left Foot*

2. Very ^ and very ^, Harry got to his feet and set off again as fast as he could without making too much noise, hurrying through the darkness back toward Hogwarts.

>   J. K. Rowling, *Harry Potter and the Goblet of Fire*

Delayed Adverbs:

3. He took a notebook out of his pocket and, ^, ^, began thumbing through it, reading notations on each page.

>   Marguerite Henry, *Misty of Chincoteague*

4. The teacher's smile shifted, ^ and ^, into a scowl that silenced the storm.

>   Katherine Paterson, *Bridge to Terabithia*

Prepositional Phrases:

5. Without ^, without ^, they savored the warm bread and shared the wine and laughed about the stranger moments of the weekend.

>   William P. Young, *The Shack*

6. We looked for it all around the house, under ^, in ^, in ^, in ^.

>   Jeannette Walls, *The Glass Castle*

Absolute Phrases:

7. They were walking in the direction of Robbie's apartment now, the leaves ^, a quarter moon ^.

    Stephen King, *UR*

8. Laughing and shoving restlessly, damp-palmed with excitement, they came shuffling into the great concrete bowl of the stadium, some ^, some ^, some ^.

    Steve Allen, "The Public Hating"

Adverb Clauses:

9. He wept until ^ , until ^ .

    William P. Young, *The Shack*

10. The Buffalo Bar sounded like a terrible place, but when ^, when ^, when ^, it seemed pretty nice.

    John Steinbeck, "Johnny Bear"

COMPOSITION: Magazine Article

Multiple tools convey rich information in articles for print or electronic magazines. This writing assignment, a magazine article, provides many opportunities for use of the sentence-composing tools, singles and multiples, within your sentences.

Pretend that you are a journalist given an assignment to write an article covering the anniversary of a traumatic historic event. In planning your article, you decide to include two kinds of information: background on the event, and a summary of the indelible memories of people about their thoughts, feelings, and experiences centered on that event. In short, the article will contain a description of the traumatic event, and the response of people to it.

For background information, research the event in print or electronic sources. For the interviews, interview three people and summarize their memories of the event.

For events in the distant past—for example, the sinking of the Titanic (1912), the explosion of the Hindenburg (1937), or the attack on Pearl Harbor (1941)—instead of live interviews, look in your research for responses of three people in the past to that traumatic event, perhaps eye-witnesses or key players.

Topic Selection

Choose any traumatic historic event that is likely to remain vividly in the minds and hearts of the people you plan to interview for your article about the event's anniversary. Here are some: *the assassination of John F. Kennedy (1963) or Martin Luther King, Jr. (1968); the Kent State University massacre (1970); the explosion of the spaceship Challenger (1986); Columbine High School massacre (1999); the terrorists' attacks on the United States on September 11 (2001); the Virginia Tech massacre (2007); or a more recent traumatic historic event.*

Begin your article with an imitation of the first paragraph of John Hersey's book *Hiroshima,* based upon the memories of people concerning another traumatic historic event, the bombing of the Japanese cities of Hiroshima and Nagasaki to end World War II. In your imitation, identify the three people whose memories you'll summarize, telling where they were when they first heard the news of the event.

Model Paragraph

At exactly fifteen minutes past eight in the morning, on August 6, 1945, Japanese time, at the moment when the atomic bomb flashed above Hiroshima, Miss Toshiko Sasaki, a clerk in the personnel department of the East Asia Tin Works, had just sat down at her place in the plant office and was turning her head to speak to the girl at the next desk. At that same moment, Dr. Fujii, a surgeon in Hiroshima, was settling down cross-legged to read the newspaper on the porch of his hospital. Mrs. Nakamura, a tailor's widow, stood by the window of her kitchen.

Sample Imitation

At approximately 1:30 in the afternoon, on November 22, 1963, Baltimore time, at the moment when the world learned of the assassination of President John Fitzgerald Kennedy, Leroy Jackson, a first-year teacher who had recently moved to Baltimore from Pennsylvania, was sorting report cards to prepare for distributing them to his homeroom at a special end-of-the-day homeroom period. At the same time, Trisha Sloan, a senior at Parkville High School who had a crush on JFK, was rehearsing a song in her choir class and was wondering why there was a commotion in the hall. Alfred Knowles, a ninth-grade student at a private school outside Chicago, was playing ping-pong in gym class. *The reaction of people to the assassination of John Fitzgerald Kennedy [**or other traumatic historic event**] is indelibly impressed upon their minds and hearts even years after the actual event.*

(Insert the italicized preview sentence at the end of your imitation paragraph to inform your reader what your magazine article is about.)

Process:

- Organize your magazine article into four parts: imitation paragraph, background information on the historic traumatic event, summary of three interviews, memorable closing paragraph.

- Research the facts to write the part of your article that summarizes what happened.

- Interview three people (or, for a distant event, research responses of three witnesses or key players).

- Begin your article with an imitation of John Hersey's paragraph (above).

- Continue your article with a few paragraphs summarizing the event, with sentences containing examples of single and multiple tools.

- Next, summarize the three interviews, with sentences containing examples of single and multiple tools.

- End the article with a dramatic paragraph that will linger in the minds of your readers, written in a style that equals the power of your first paragraph (an imitation), but this time without imitating a model.

- Give your article a title (the name of the event) and a subtitle (a brief comment about that event) separated with a colon. *(Example: "The Assassination of President Kennedy: An Unhealed Wound")*

"It is unrealistic to expect that you can bleach the trauma out of your mind. Learn how to cope with the experience and with the memories, and to live in the present."
—Lisa Lewis, poet

Mixed Tools

In each pair, the second sentence has mixed tools. Notice how the mixed tools add detail and style to the sentence.

1a. Phyllis was with her father when her mother called her to come and see Neil Armstrong set foot on the moon.

1b. **Concerned with her father, who lay dying in the bedroom, but not wanting to miss the moon landing,** Phyllis was with her father when her mother called her to come and see Neil Armstrong set foot on the moon. *(past participial phrase, adjective clause, present participial phrase)*

        Frank McCourt, *Teacher Man*

2a. Huston spoke to his committee.

2b. Huston, **a tall spare man, wind-blackened, with eyes like little blades,** spoke to his committee, **one man from each sanitary unit.** *(appositive phrase, past participial phrase, prepositional phrase, appositive phrase)*

        John Steinbeck, *The Grapes of Wrath*

3a. There they all were now.

3b. There they all were now, **the cream of the school, the lights and leaders of the senior class, with their high I.Q.'s and expensive shoes, pasting each other with snowballs.** *(two appositive phrases, prepositional phrase, present participial phrase)*

        John Knowles, *A Separate Peace*

4a. I suppressed it.

4b. **Viciously,** I suppressed it, **fighting against the equally sharp lash of agony, as my eyes continued to the face beneath the black hair, the face that wasn't the one I wanted to see.** *(opening adverb, present participial phrase, adverb clause, appositive phrase)*

        Stephenie Meyer, *New Moon*

Reviewing the Sentence-Composing Toolbox

WHAT ARE MIXED TOOLS? *They are two or more different tools within the same sentence.*

Mixed tools can occur anywhere within the sentence—together or apart.

Examples:

Together: I sniffed and wiped my stupid tears, **trying to pull myself together, because that girl was back, the plump one in pink.** *(present participial phrase, adverb clause, appositive phrase)*

Sara Gruen, *Water for Elephants*

Apart: **After the tyrannosaur's head crashed against the hood of the Land Cruiser and shattered the windshield,** Tim was knocked flat on the seat, **his mouth warm with blood.** *(adverb clause, absolute phrase)*

Michael Crichton, *Jurassic Park*

In the practices with mixed tools, you will be working with all of the sentence-composing tools in this worktext. To review any of them, study the page indicated.

NOUN GROUP: THE NAMING TOOLS

He looked out a window at the silent small-town street, **a street he had never seen until yesterday.**

Truman Capote, *In Cold Blood*

Dumping the armload of firewood into the woodbox made the sleepers stir but not wake.

Toni Morrison, *Beloved*

He tried **to think what else he might have touched.**

Cormac McCarthy, *No Country for Old Men*

What he said was true.

Virginia Woolf, *To the Lighthouse*

212

VERB GROUP: THE NARRATING TOOLS

In four huge steps, the tyrannosaur **covered the distance to the goat, bent down,** and **bit it through the neck.**

Michael Crichton, *Jurassic Park*

In the town, in little offices, **sat the men who bought pearls from the fishermen.**

John Steinbeck, *The Pearl*

ADJECTIVE GROUP: THE DESCRIBING TOOLS

Speechless, Bryson scanned the small living room, frantically.

Robert Ludlum, *The Prometheus Deception*

After a few months, I went on with the business of my life, **certain that my career as an author would be short-lived,** but glad to have survived the publishing process with my dignity more or less intact.

Barack Obama, *Dreams from My Father*

Picking his way down a narrow gorge, Mortenson stepped off ice and onto solid ground for the first time in more than three months.

Greg Mortenson and David Oliver Relin, *Three Cups of Tea*

In the following months, **dismayed at how difficult it was to carry a heavy cello that half mile to school,** I switched to the more portable flute.

Perri Knize, *A Piano Odyssey*

Tommy's large nose, **with no hair above,** looked larger.

Tracy Kidder, *Home Town*

Carefully taking the burning match from his friend's fingertips, he set it in the bowl, and soon we had a fire **to toast our palms and fingertips.**

Keith Donohue, *The Stolen Child*

My mother appeared in the doorway, **her eyes two warnings.**

Tracy Chevalier, *Girl with a Pearl Earring*

She failed to see a shadow, **which followed her like her own shadow, which stopped when she stopped,** and **which started again when she did.**

Gaston Leroux, *The Phantom of the Opera*

ADVERB GROUP: THE EXPLAINING TOOLS

Hesitantly, I reached out one finger and stroked the back of his shimmering hand, where it lay within my reach.

Stephenie Meyer, *Twilight*

Then the creeping murderer, the octopus, steals out, moving like a gray mist, pretending now to be a bit of weed, now a rock, now a lump of decaying meat while its evil goat eyes watch, **coldly.**

John Steinbeck, *Cannery Row*

On the ridge, the snow was melting in spots.

Albert Camus, "The Guest"

The heavy bag for boxers is for power, **to build up fighters' arms and shoulders.**

Robert Lipsyte, *The Contender*

In pregnancy she seemed to him beautiful but fragile, **fine blue veins faintly visible through her pale white skin.**

Kim Edwards, The Memory Keeper's Daughter

Before the girls got to the porch, I heard their laughter crackling and popping like pine logs in a cooking stove.

Maya Angelou, I Know Why the Caged Bird Sings

PRACTICE 1: MATCHING AND IMITATING

This practice focuses on mixed tools in the *opening position*. Match the mixed tools with the sentence. Write out the sentence, and then imitate it. Name the mixed tools in the model and your imitation.

Sentences:

1. ^, they crossed the porch and descended the other step to the lawn.

   Wallace Stegner, *Crossing to Safety*

2. ^, Webster combined the musical charm of his deep organ-like voice, a vivid imagination, an ability to crush his opponents with a barrage of facts, a confident and deliberate manner of speaking and a striking appearance, to make his orations a magnet that drew crowds.

   John F. Kennedy, *Profiles in Courage*

3. ^, he surveyed the goings-on through a scrim of cynicism.

   Anne Tyler, *The Amateur Marriage*

Opener Mix:

a. a very slow speaker, averaging hardly a hundred words a minute

b. grave and solicitous, intensely concentrated

c. at parties, when all six-foot-five of him thundered into the room

4. ^, the two dogs were stretched, their dripping tongues covered with dust.

    John Steinbeck, *The Grapes of Wrath*

    d. in the red dust under the truck, panting

5. ^, attention shifted to him like sunflowers turning to the sun.

    Khaled Hosseini, *The Kite Runner*

    e. slumped glumly on Anna's piano bench before the meal, his arms folded, his chin on his chest

PRACTICE 2: EXPANDING

Partner with the author by creating mixed tools for the *opening position*. Use any mixed tools.

1. ^, ^, there was a gravel road all grown in with weeds.

    Stephen King, *Everything's Eventual*

2. ^, and ^, I wanted to run away and be gone from this strange place.

    Keith Donohue, *The Stolen Child*

3. ^, ^, she was just a few months out of college, and serious adulthood still seemed a far distant concept.

    John Grogan, *Marley & Me*

4. ^, ^, Sandy Glass smiled most when he was angry.

    Allegra Goodman, *Intuition*

5. ^, ^, I stood on the hill on the left.

    Yann Martel, *Life of Pi*

PRACTICE 3: MATCHING AND IMITATING

This practice focuses on mixed tools in the *S-V split position*. Match the mixed tools with the sentence. Write out the sentence, and then imitate it. Name the mixed tools in the model and your imitation.

Sentences:

1. Forty people, ^, nearly filled the little chapel.

   Charles Frazier, *Cold Mountain*

2. Sergeant Fales, ^, felt anger with the pain.

   Mark Bowden, *Black Hawk Down*

3. At about four o'clock in the afternoon, the car, ^, drove up to the Smith house.

   Fannie Flagg, *Standing in the Rainbow*

4. A framed picture of Prime Minister Jawaharlal Nehru, ^, hung opposite Ghosh's chair.

   Abraham Verghese, *Cutting for Stone*

5. The canoe, ^, twisted and shifted in the rushing waters.

   Armstrong Sperry, *Call It Courage*

S-V Split Mix:

a. dressed in black, somber

b. a dusty old four-door green Packard, packed full of people, songbooks, and clothes, and sound equipment piled up on the top and on the running boards

c. stripped of sail and mast, without a paddle

d. a big broad-faced man, who had fought in Panama and during the Gulf War

e. handsome and pensive, one finger on his cheek

PRACTICE 4: EXPANDING

Partner with the author by creating mixed tools for the *S-V split position*. Use any mixed tools.

1. Her husband, ^, ^, tried hard to make her happy.
   Sherwood Anderson, *Winesburg, Ohio*

2. The great white bed, ^, ^, almost filled the little shadowy room.
   Joan Aiken, "Searching for Summer"

3. A great book, ^, ^, demands the most active reading of which you are capable.
   Mortimer Adler, "How to Mark a Book"

4. One of his faculty colleagues, ^, ^, had observed to him that the college made you feel like an eighteenth-century live-in tutor, responsible for educating the children of an English lord.
   Robert Ludlum, *The Prometheus Deception*

5. His teeth, ^ and ^, were still intact.
   Truman Capote, *In Cold Blood*

PRACTICE 5: MATCHING AND IMITATING

This practice focuses on mixed tools in the *closer position*. Match the mixed tools with the sentence. Write out the sentence, and then imitate it. Name the mixed tools in the model and your imitation.

Sentences:

1. Then the face appeared before her, ^.
   Stephen King, *The Dead Zone*

2. There is a spider, ^.
   Annie Dillard, "Death of a Moth"

3. Boo drifted to a corner of the room, ^.
   Harper Lee, *To Kill a Mockingbird*

Closer Mix:

a. my coat and tie flung over a chair, surrounded by soul food and love

b. in the bathroom, of uncertain lineage, bulbous at the abdomen and drab, whose six-inch mess of web works, miraculously, to keep her alive and me amazed

c. panting, the corded vein in his forehead inflamed

4. He slumped against a wall, ^.

   Carson McCullers, *The Heart Is a Lonely Hunter*

d. floating in the darkness, a horrible face out of a nightmare

5. It was good to sit there in Charley's kitchen, ^.

   Eugenia Collier, "Sweet Potato Pie"

e. where he stood with his chin up, peering from a distance at Jem

PRACTICE 6: EXPANDING

Partner with the author by creating mixed tools for the *closer position*. Use any mixed tools.

1. The men found Rosie the elephant lying on her side, ^, ^.

   Sara Gruen, *Water for Elephants*

2. He felt stupid for having been lured inside, ^, ^.

   Neil Gaiman, *The Graveyard Book*

3. Some ants got out of the fire, ^, and ^.

   Ernest Hemingway, *A Farewell to Arms*

4. He turned to face his sleeping grandson, ^, ^.

   Jhumpa Lahiri, *Unaccustomed Earth*

5. Andy Schmeikl walked across and studied her, ^ and ^, ^.

   Markus Zusak, *The Book Thief*

PRACTICE 7: MATCHING AND IMITATING

This practice focuses on mixed tools in *various positions within the sentence*. Match the mixed tools with the sentence. Write out the sentence, and then imitate it. Name the mixed tools in the model and your imitation.

Sentences:

1. ^, there were moments when he believed ^.

    Anne Tyler, *Saint Maybe*

2. ^, the sailors caught an enormous shark, ^.

    Isabel Allende, *Daughter of Fortune*

3. ^, she could see the heavy uniformed man, ^.

    Lois Lowry, *Number the Stars*

4 ^, they returned to the car lot, ^.

    Mitch Albom, *The Five People You Meet in Heaven*

5. ^, his wife, ^, leaned out of the window, ^.

    Bernard Malamud, "A Summer's Reading"

Mix in Various Positions:

a. amazingly / that someday, somehow, he was going to end up famous

b. while he was reading the paper / a fat woman with a white face / gazing into the street, her thick white arms folded on the window ledge under her loose breasts

c. at midmorning / which died on deck, thrashing wickedly in its death throes, while no one dared go near enough to club it

d. later, when it was dark / exhausted and laughing, drinking beer from brown paper bags

e. from her hiding place in the narrow sliver of open doorway / a holstered pistol at his waist, in the entrance to the kitchen, peering in toward the sink

PRACTICE 8: EXPANDING

Partner with the author by creating mixed tools for *various positions within the sentence*. Use any mixed tools.

1. A child, ^, grinned at me, ^.

    > Stephenie Meyer, *New Moon*

2. ^, Gramps was thrown out of high school for ^.

    > Barack Obama, *Dreams from My Father*

3. ^, Chicago is America's city, ^.

    > Alex Kotlowitz, *Never a City So Real*

4. ^, he stood there like he was in shock, ^, and then ^.

    > Jeannette Walls, *The Glass Castle*

5. What matters ^ is what you ^, not how you ^.

    > Isabel Allende, *Daughter of Fortune*

COMPOSITION: News Report

ASSIGNMENT: In covering the news, journalists strive to provide detailed information about a story. Using mixed sentence-composing tools is one way to provide those details. For this paper, pretend you covered a crime scene and took four written notes at the scene of the crime, made many mental notes about details at the scene of the crime, and now are ready to write the story, <u>with mixed tools to provide lots of details</u>.

Journalist's Notes:

1. ^, the detective ^ found only one clue ^.
2. ^, his partner ^ stood over the body ^.
3. ^, a crime lab professional worked around them ^.
4. ^, a single bystander ^ watched everything ^.

The following examples show some of the types of tools you can add for information about the detective for the first sentence above.

Examples:

Appositive phrase—A cracker-jack crime scene investigator known for his intuitive savvy, the detective found only one clue.

Present participial phrase—Combing the scene in his usual thorough manner, the detective found only one clue.

Past participial phrase—Stumped by the unique puzzle this particular crime scene presented, the detective found only one clue.

Absolute phrase—His face wearing a perplexed expression unprecedented for this master sleuth, the detective found only one clue.

Prepositional phrase—In the vicinity of the victim's body, the detective found only one clue.

Infinitive phrase—To conceal his secret role as conspirator in the crime, the detective found only one clue.

Adverb clause—After he searched the scene of the crime and analyzed the position of the body, the detective found only one clue.

Process:

■ Expand each of the four sentence-notes by adding mixed tools in the slots indicated by carets (^).

■ Immediately following each of those four sentences, add an original sentence using your choice of tools: one telling more about the detective; one telling more about his partner; one telling more about the crime lab professional, one telling more about the bystander.

■ Include a variety of types of sentence-composing tools. You can review all of them on pages 195–221.

■ When you finish, your news report of the crime scene will have eight sentences: four from the above activity, alternating with four of your own.

■ Create a headline for your news story about the crime scene investigation.

Variety is the spice of life (and sentences).

Writing unfolds one sentence at a time. Sentences unfold one part at a time. The most important parts of well-built sentences are the additions. Good writing results from those additions.

"Composition is essentially a process of <u>addition</u>."
—Francis Christensen, "A Generative Rhetoric of the Sentence"

Additions generate sentence power through elaboration via the sentence-composing tools, used in singles, multiples, and mixes. *Grammar for College Writing: A Sentence-Composing Approach* focuses on those additions—the tools for elaboration. Good writers use them to build their sentences. Now, you can, too.

"Give us the tools and we will finish the job."
—Sir Winston Churchill, British prime minister

In a piece of writing between 750 and 1,000 words, demonstrate your skill in using those sentence-composing tools.

COMPOSITION: Process Essay

ASSIGNMENT: Think about a technical or nontechnical process you know a lot about, perhaps more than most people. Then draft and revise an essay for educated adult readers explaining how that process works, happens, occurs, or functions.

Topic Selection

Choose a topic for your essay that will benefit your readers by providing new or improved knowledge or understanding of the process.

Examples:

How a human heart functions

How the confirmation process for Supreme Court nominees works

How prejudice works

How a hurricane forms

How a baby is born

How the circulatory or respiratory system works

How inflation works

How an IRS income tax audit is conducted

How a computer's memory functions

How a child becomes an adult

How HTML language works

How the stock market operates

How society favors attractive people

How a terrorist is born

How leaves turn color in the fall

How a recession in the economy happens

How spyware or viruses get into your computer

How an eating disorder like anorexia or bulimia develops

How a digital camera works

How laughter promotes physical and emotional health

How DNA is replicated

How fame victimizes celebrities

How an iPod works (See sample essay on pages 226–28.)

Special Feature

For a captivating opening paragraph, imitate this model, adding your thesis sentence at the end. The purpose of a thesis sentence is to preview the process your essay will be explaining.

Model Paragraph

This is a snail shell, round, full, and glossy as a horse chestnut. Comfortable and compact, it sits curled up like a cat in the hollow of my hand. Milky and opaque, it has the pinkish bloom of the sky on a summer evening, ripening to rain. On its smooth, symmetrical face is penciled with precision a perfect spiral, winding inward to the pinpoint center of the shell, the tiny dark core of the apex, the pupil of the eye. *[Add a thesis sentence here to preview your essay for your readers.]*

Anne Morrow Lindberg, *Gift from the Sea*

Sample Imitation

He is a newborn babe, fresh, beautiful, and playful as a puppy. Comfortable and trusting, he rests peacefully with his pacifier on the bosom of his mother's chest. Smiling and gentle, he has the eyes of his mother, glowing with innocence. On his adorable, sweet face is reflected by genetics a facsimile, blending closely the biological composition of his parents, the genetic structure of Mom and Dad, a DNA road map. *What his parents don't realize is that already taking place is an on-going process inside his tiny body called DNA replication (thesis sentence).*

Process:

- Begin with an imitation of the model paragraph, ending with a thesis sentence previewing what your essay will be about.

- Using knowledge from personal experience, reading, or the Internet, draft several paragraphs clearly explaining the process.

- Select information and details that will educate, enlighten, inform, or even entertain your readers about the process to increase their knowledge and understanding.

- Avoid an overly technical style so that the process will be understandable by nontechnical but educated readers.

- Expand early drafts of the essay by adding numerous and varied sentence-composing tools for details of the process you are explaining.

- Provide a clever, original title.

- End your essay with a memorable paragraph as good as the first paragraph of your essay—without imitating a model.

"You'll never get anywhere with all those damn little short sentences."
—Gregory Clark, *A Social Perspective on the Function of Writing*

Here are two versions of a sample process essay: an early draft without tools (231 words) and the final draft with tools (792 words). *Seventy-one percent of the final draft is provided through the sentence-composing tools.*

"iBaby Maybe" (early draft)

This is an iPod. It lodges easily in the case on my belt like a deck of playing cards. It stores in its small container incredible amounts of digitized music and video. On the iPod's sleek, smooth front is designed with efficiency a simple touch-control. *The iPod is an ever-evolving ubiquitous device that interfaces with your computer and the Internet to provide audio and video entertainment. (thesis sentence)*

First install the iTunes program onto your computer. The iTunes software is easy to install. Click on "Download iTunes," choose your operating system (Mac or PC), and the iTunes program hurls through cyberspace to your computer.

The software has a link to the iTunes Store. Apple provides the software for free. The route is smooth.

The iTunes Store is the source for virtually any tune. The iTunes Store website is easily navigated.

The fun begins. Your entire library of music and video is automatically transferred to the device. The iTunes programming will "synch" your iPod.

The iPod has become the tech gadget of the age. Walkman portables quickly became obsolete.

The name "iPod" struck gold. The iPod has gone through a number of generations.

A device like the iPod would have been unthinkable.

Babies shortly after birth may have a tiny device implanted in their brains. The tiny tech tot will be a little bundle of joy. *(231 words)*

---

*"It doesn't matter how you write the first draft or even the second draft, but it makes all the difference in the world **how you write the final draft.**"*
—Elizabeth White, author

"iBaby Maybe" (final draft, with additions in **boldface**)

This is an iPod, **digital, small, and compact as a cell phone. Light-weight and attractive**, it lodges easily in the case on my belt like a deck of playing cards. **Amazing and efficient**, it stores in its small container incredible amounts of digitized music and video. On the iPod's sleek, smooth front is designed with efficiency a simple touch-control, **providing access to its operation, the digital command center, the key to my tunes.** *A **technological marvel**, the iPod is an ever-evolving ubiquitous device that interfaces with your computer and the Internet to provide audio and video entertainment. (thesis sentence)*

To use your new iPod, first install the iTunes program onto your computer. **Available as a free download, for either Macintosh or PC,** the iTunes software is easy to install, **taking only a few mouse clicks, with no snags or surprises.**

From Apple's website, click on "Download iTunes," choose your operating system (Mac or PC), and the iTunes program hurls through cyberspace to your computer, **an incredible digital entertainment package only seconds away.**

The software has a link to the iTunes Store, **the reason for the free download. To get an instant huge client base, to capture a huge market share of the home entertainment industry, including all types of music and video, to establish a virtual monopoly for easy and instant acquisition of entertainment media without having to visit a big box store,** Apple provides, **irresistibly and instantly,** the software for free. **From the iTunes Store to your computer to your iPod**, the route is smooth, **easy, and quick.**

A vast music and video store in cyberspace, owned and operated by Apple, Inc., the iTunes Store is the source for virtually any tune, **in any category imaginable, from rock to opera, and any film or TV video. Attractive in design and easy to use, a virtual one-stop home entertainment center a mouse click away,** the iTunes Store website is easily navigated, **even by first-timers, for accessing information about songs or albums, films or TV shows, and reading user reviews with a five-star rating system, and, of course, purchasing and downloading tunes, videos, podcasts, and applications.**

With the iTunes software on your computer, the fun begins, **including making libraries of music imported from CDs or other electronic means, customizing playlists to include songs of any category imaginable, like "Jogging Tunes," "Oldies but Goodies," "Romantic Vibes," "Biggest Hits of Superstars," or any collection that can be imported from the library of tunes stored on your computer. When your iPod is connected to your computer,** your entire library of music and video, **including your custom playlists,** is automatically transferred to the device, **effortlessly and quickly.** The iTunes programming, **sensitive to changes,** will, **immediately and automatically,** "synch" your iPod, **to update the device's contents by adding to your iPod new music or video you've added to your computer, updating the device since the last time you connected your iPod to your computer.**

First introduced by Apple in 2001, the iPod has become the tech gadget of the age, consumers of all ages around the world flocking to buy the new storage device for their music, replacing almost immediately the up-until-then popular Sony product, the Walkman, a portable cassette recorder that allowed people to listen to music via headphones larger than iPod earbuds. Because the iPod, unlike the Walkman, allowed for storage of digitized music within its box—instead of having to carry cassette tapes containing the music, Walkman portables quickly became obsolete, **as did the cassettes that had been the mainstream media for recorded music.**

Based upon mention of a pod in the space film *2001: A Space Odyssey*, the name "iPod," **instantly memorable**, struck gold, **starting a whole line of iThings like iMacs, iPhones, iPads, and others.** Since its introduction, the iPod has gone through a number of generations, **each adding new and remarkable features like Podcasts, which are downloadable spoken texts of every conceivable stripe, including foreign language lessons, university lectures, radio and TV broadcasts, spoken word audio books, and more.**

In the nontech past, a device like the iPod, **small, reliable, affordable, storing thousands of songs and playing them through tiny speakers inserted into your ears while you jog, walk, or just sit and groove on the music,** would have been unthinkable.

In a sci-fi future, as the iPod shrinks to microscopic size, although unthinkable now, babies shortly after birth may have a tiny device implanted in their brains. **Unable even to crawl,** the tiny tech tot will be a little bundle of joy, **the joy emanating from its iBrain, where the baby's choices might be "Rock-a-Bye, Baby" for sleeping sweetly, and then, for waking rousingly, "We Will Rock You"—plus, for in between, every tune ever recorded, playable on demand by the iBaby.** Maybe? *(792 words—seventy-one percent provided through the sentence-composing tools)*

About Good Sentences

1. What is the grammar of a sentence?

   A complete sentence must have a subject and predicate, but also often additions.

2. What's an *addition*?

   It's a sentence part built by one of the twenty-one tools in this worktext to add elaboration.

3. What is a *good sentence*?

   It's one like the author's sentence models in this worktext. Open any page for examples.

4. Why are those sentences *good*?

   A sentence is good if its content is interesting or informative or insightful or original—and therefore memorable, good if the way the content is expressed uses the kinds of tools in this worktext.

5. What's the best way to write a sentence like that?

   Create a sentence blueprint, and then, using tools from this worktext, build the sentence. If you build a sentence with quality materials (thoughts) and power tools (the grammatical structures of authors), it will be good. People will read it—and maybe remember it because they learn from it or enjoy it or admire it, perhaps even love it.

6. Why write good sentences?

   Pulitzer Prize writer Barbara Tuchman has the answer: "When it comes to language, nothing is more satisfying than to write a good sentence."